The Great Festival

The Great Festival presents and analyzes two historical festivals – the ancient Dionysus Festival and the present Roskilde Festival. The purpose is to set up two comparable structures or "codes" to explain the universal artistic effects, structures, and fascination of the festival.

Olav Harsløf argues that there are major structural, organizational, and economic similarities that, when exposed, can give us greater insight into today's festivals. This is illuminated through a combined performance design and event analysis of the ancient Dionysus Festival and today's Roskilde Festival, explaining the festival's historicity, diversity, complexity, and paradigmatic strength.

This will be a discussion of great interest to researchers and students in the fields of performance studies, experience economy, theater, music, classical philology, and archeology.

Olav Harsløf is a former professor at the Department of Performance Design, Roskilde University, Denmark, and before that was Head of the Danish National Academy of Theatre, and the Danish National Conservatory of Rhythmic Music. He has, together with Dorita Hannah, edited the book *Performance Design* (2008) and written the article "*PH*antom of the Operas in Sydney and Copenhagen"; and together with Erik Kristiansen he has edited the book *Engaging Spaces – Sites of Performance, Interaction and Reflection* (2015) and written the article "Space as Provocation."

The Great Festival

A Theoretical Performance Narrative of Antiquity's Feasts and the Modern Rock Festival

Olav Harsløf

Translated from the Danish
by Kenny Sanders

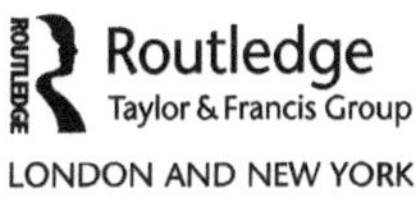

LONDON AND NEW YORK

First published 2020
by Routledge
2 Park Square, Milton Park, Abingdon, Oxon OX14 4RN

and by Routledge
605 Third Avenue, New York, NY 10017

First issued in paperback 2021

Routledge is an imprint of the Taylor & Francis Group, an informa business

British Library Cataloguing-in-Publication Data
A catalogue record for this book is available from the British Library

Library of Congress Cataloging-in-Publication Data
A catalog record for this book has been requested

ISBN 13: 978-1-03-223782-4 (pbk)
ISBN 13: 978-0-367-20495-2 (hbk)

Typeset in Baskerville
by Apex CoVantage, LLC

Contents

Preface

In 2000 I became the leader of a project to initiate Denmark's Museum of Rock Music and Culture, and during subsequent board work, I felt the desire to uncover or analyze what one might call "a universal festival structure." By investigating and analyzing ancient Greek Dionysian feasts as well as today's Danish Roskilde Festival, I wanted to seek out and present comparative models or "codes" that might explain the festivals' universal agencies, structures, and power to fascinate.

I chose to approach this material in an extremely concrete manner. In October 2009, I visited Attica, the Peloponnesian Islands, and Naples to study the ruins of many of antiquity's theaters, squares, sports arenas, and cities. The purpose of this trip was to examine the architectural space of these ruins, their anthropology, organization, and structures and to show how these features would be repeated in future epochs' modern festivals. During the next two years, these investigations were followed up by, all together, six months of research at the Danish Institute and the Nordic library in Athens. I have also been attending and participating in northern Europe's largest rock festival, the Roskilde Festival, for more than a decade.

Theoretically, methodologically, and analytically, my book is oriented toward a theoretical performance analysis, and my specific goal has been to analyze and define ancient feasts and the modern rock festival's "performative space." Even though performance theory is now almost 60 years old, it still only receives limited acceptance as a scientific theory and analytical method by the traditional humanist academy. Despite the prevailing opposition between "old" and "new" humanities, performance theory has especially achieved gains in the theater, art, and design sciences but has also created entire new areas of study such as Performance Studies, Performance Design and Humanistic Technology, or Art and Technology. Most critical of performance theory, not to say dismissive, has been classic philology, as well as parts of the literature, history, and music sciences – institutionalized knowledge traditions that still have a strained relationship to older "new" subject area constructions such as Sociology, Anthropology, Film & Media Science, and Communication Studies. I am critical of these attitudes and positions in my book with the hope of accelerating a discussion that could lead to necessary theoretical clarifications, scientific cooperation, and progress.

But first and foremost, it has been a great pleasure to introduce a new genre, *the festival* – and particularly in the context of this book, the modern music festival – into the field of science and submit it to an analysis based on the most prominent theories in the field. For me, the most obvious and relevant conceptual apparatus for making this analysis is, without a doubt, performance science.

Introduction

Festival Myths:

"A classic tragedy"

In the year 458 BCE at Athens's wooden theater on the south slope of the Acropolis, the spectators' tribune collapsed during a performance of the playwright Aeschylus's tragedy Agamemnon. *The calamity was so extensive that the Athenian popular assembly chose to bring the case to trial. Aeschylus was declared guilty and sent into exile to Sicily where he, in great bitterness, spent the last two years of his life, never passing up an opportunity to condemn the popular assembly. At the same time, the assembly learned from the accident, in the sense that they constructed a solid foundation made of stone and wooden beams beneath the Athens's theater space. More than a hundred years later, this was replaced by a marble theater in the same location.*

In the year 2000 CE, nine spectators were crushed and trampled to death during a Pearl Jam concert at Roskilde Festival's Orange Stage on the livestock fairgrounds just south of Roskilde, Denmark. The accident was so extensive that the police initiated an investigation into the episode, initially dividing the guilt equally between the band and the festival's leadership. After a second look, these charges were dropped. In the meantime, the band chose to go into voluntary exile, vowing never again to play at the Roskilde Festival, but at the same time they never passed up an opportunity to condemn the festival's leaders. Meanwhile, after researching the accident, the festival's leadership chose to invest a large amount into security equipment the very next year.

NOTE: Both events are still strongly debated, though myth and reality get mixed up in the various versions.

Dionysus at Roskilde?

Festival and carnival

Denmark is the land of great festivals. The largest is the *Roskilde Festival,* a rock music festival, which takes place every year for ten days at the beginning of July with 65–90,000 participants. The next largest festival is the *Copenhagen Jazz Festival,* which takes place annually right after the Roskilde Festival in July. Here, 200,000 tickets are sold, bought by an estimated 50–60,000 people.

In April each year there is also a *Children's Theater Festival,* hosted for one week by varying Danish municipalities. In the 1980s during Whitsun, downtown Copenhagen was converted to a veritable *Carnival.* This immediately developed into a "city-wide" party, with damaged cars and broken shop windows, and was therefore relegated to the capital city's large public parks just outside the city center. In one of the country's provincial towns, *Carnival* still takes place in the heart of the city and with undiminished vigor.

The Whitsun carnival originally drew its structural inspiration from festival forms developed during the Middle Ages and the Renaissance. It grew out of central and southern European city carnival structures then continued to develop, incorporating South American performance forms like music and dance festivals. Today, to a great degree, the Danish Whitsun Carnival has embraced the tone and form of rock music festivals, and can be considered a hybrid.

Performance design

In my field, Performance Design, we employ art forms' aesthetics, anthropology, production, and organization. We study their means of expression (musically, dramatically, architecturally, and visually), their forms (stage, sculpture, installation, surface, space, light), and their audience. But we also study organizational structures (political, administrative, regarding craft, and personnel) and forms of production (construction, process, design).

The theme of this book is "The Great Festival," which we know historically from descriptions of Dionysian feasts – their structure, architectural space, anthropology, and organization – and the ancient Greek festival structure – which has been repeated in later epochs' festivals from the middle ages to modern times. With this work I would like to show that a number of structures, for more than two thousand years, have been maintained from the Dionysian feasts right through to our own contemporary Danish rock festival. For a long time it's been clear to me that these festivals have more in common than differences, and that one can talk of a "universal concept" developed in classical Greece.

Theoretics and methodologies

My analysis takes its starting point from performance research's theoretic founders Victor Turner and Richard Schechner's studies and theoretical formations that they began to develop in the 1960s. Since that time the institutionalization of their anthropological and dramaturgical work has spawned a great deal of scientific literature that has re-analyzed a long list of classic fields of study – theater, music, dance, visual art, architecture, linguistics, philosophy, rhetoric, history, sociology, anthropology, cultural, and social history and sport – and newer fields such as psychology, pedagogy, health science, communication, and information technology, computer science, information and library science, experience economics, gastronomy, and a number of modern art, cultural, and gender studies. Among Turner and Schechner's heirs that have had great significance for me, I would like to name Barbara Kirshenblatt-Gimblett, Marvin Carlson, Jon McKenzie (USA), Erica Fischer-Lichte (Germany), Gay McAuley (Australia), Dorita Hannah (New Zealand), Kathleen Irwin (Canada), Simon Frith (England) and Jørgen Østergård Andersen (Denmark).

It is my thesis that there are internal connections among a number of art forms, myths, and rituals, as well as natural scientific thought and practice. I will illuminate and expand this thesis through a combination of performance, design and event analysis of the ancient Dionysian Festival and today's Roskilde Festival in an attempt to explain "the festival's" historicity, diversity, complexity, and paradigmatic strength.

What is a festival?

The word festival is new to most continental European languages and seems to be one of many English words that made it across the Channel in the 1950s and 1960s. Foreign dictionaries and modern lexicons note this as well telling us that the word comes from English, was formed from the Latin *festivalis*, then adjectivized to *festum* (feast or feast day). The meaning, however, is somewhat closer to "like a feast day." The word wandered from France to England in the 18th century then back again in the 19th – now with the meaning "large German music festival," then later also English and French music festivals were included. In 1878, the French Academy accepted the word as a neologism (Autissier 2009:21).

The *Cambridge Dictionary* gives us a double definition of festival:

1 a special day or period, usually in memory of a religious event with its own social activities, food, or ceremonies;
and:
2 an organized set of special events, such as musical performances.

The Great Danish Encyclopedia, on the other hand, ventures into a more precise determination of the phenomenon as a

> cultural arrangement, that is most often periodic and recurring and extends over several days. During festivals, single or several forms of performative art are presented, like music, dance, film or theater, often with greatly varied and combined offerings, but now and then devoted to one special theme. Festivals representing a single artist (for example Richard Wagner's Bayreuth pageant from 1876) are a special exception. Festivals are preferably tied to a single town. Here, national and international audiences are offered a concentrated program, that separates itself from other cultural events that might take place during the year, for example, with famous artists as attractions or with presentations of new or lesser known art. There can be significant commercial interests in festivals.
>
> The Dionysian festival in ancient Athens can be seen as a forerunner to the modern festival: here, in a religious context, comedies and tragedies were performed from morning to evening for four days. The concept of recurring artistic events that reach out to large audiences, can be found once again in the middle ages' yearly mystery and passion plays, and again in the 1800s, especially in the German language festival tradition where theater performances marked a (local) historic event, preferably outdoors and with active participation of the local populace (see open air theaters).

There is some misleading information here and several things are mixed together, like concerts, pageants, religious festivals, city festivals, musicals, dance performances, and film. In addition to this, "pageants" that celebrate one composer are absolutely not unusual. Plus, Dionysian festivals can hardly be called "religious." And they lasted not four days but eight, with choir music, dance, sport, recitations, comedies, and satyr plays.

The "festival" label isn't, as opposed to "comedy," "novel," or "circus," a generally well-defined category. It is used in a variety of ways, as in the quoted encyclopedia article – or even more broadly: wine festivals, beer festivals, apple festivals, shellfish festivals etc. In festival research, which in 2004 established the European Festival Research Project (EFRP) with support from several national funds and advisory committees, the classical musical festival tradition since the 1720s has been positioned as the foundation for modern festival development. Though in the foreword to the project's anthology *The Europe of Festivals. From Zagreb to Edinburgh, Intersecting Viewpoints,* the musician and director of the international Aix-en-Provence Festival, Bernard Foccroulle, attempted to fix the baseline for this tradition in antiquity and the middle ages:

> Since the end of WW2 festivals have multiplied in Europe just as monasteries and cathedrals burgeoned in the Middle Ages.
>
> (Foccroulle 2009:11)

> One is aware of the thread linking festivals to the tradition of Greek theatre that gathered crowds around magnificent texts and shows combining popular festivities and thorough thinking over the meaning of life.
>
> (Foccroulle 2009:16)

After this, Foccroulle lists classical music festivals both in Europe and worldwide that he himself had participated in through the last fifty years.

In an outline of the festivals' historical progress and development over 250 years, the anthology's editor Anne-Marie Autissier, sustains this point of view. It is first in the section labeled: "1960–1980: Contemporary Creations, the Establishment of Minority Cultures, and the Multiplication of Music Styles" (Autissier 2009:31) that new types of festivals are discussed – "free and entertaining events" with dance, poetry, theater and new music forms like jazz and rock. She formulates it like this: "After the famous festival housed on the Isle of Wight in 1968 many rock music events climbed on the bandwagon" (Autissier 2009:32–33). Then English, Swiss, and Belgian rock festivals are named. The large north European rock festivals of the 80s, 90s and into the new century aren't mentioned. The article's subsequent focus is directed toward – folklore, women and minority culture festivals – mostly discussing these festivals' economy and tourist potential.

Anne-Marie Autissier, like a number of the anthology's additional contributors, sees the growth of festivals since WWII as, in an international context, active peace making. Here national contradictions and aversions are reconciled through cultural gatherings. And she sees the great boom in East European festivals after the "wall's fall" in 1989 as a confirmation of this. She also sees festivals as great potential employers:

> As a conclusion converging lines in the area of festivals can be drawn through their history: creating or re-creating public spaces, federating scattered audiences, asserting values or ideologies and always creating employment for artists.
>
> (Autissier 2009:39)

In addition to this, Anne-Marie Autissier focuses on the festival's form, dissemination, and diversity. Though the concept of festival is not defined or separated from categories such as "trade fairs," "exhibitions," "concert series," or "shows." Most conspicuous though is that the audience is neither presented nor their needs analyzed.

On the other hand, this also happens in several other publications about this subject (Munkgård Pedersen 2010), and by the Roskilde Festival's architect Jes Vagnby in *Temporary Architecture and Physical Planning for the Roskilde Festival* (2010):

> Many visit the festival [Roskilde Festival] to experience the great artistic offerings, but equally, to be challenged by meeting with others, and by either participating in or observing the social culture that arises when many different people gather together, free from the obligations of their everyday lives.
>
> This challenge, that festival participants can experience within themselves, is about the surrendering and letting go of inhibitions, allowing oneself to be pulled into the festival's experiences and atmosphere. This is a fight between the planned and organized, and the unforeseen and accidental. It is a fight between control and chaos.
>
> For the individual festival participant, the Roskilde Festival encompasses important social and psychological challenges that stimulate the individual participant's senses and that dares one to engage, get involved and to set oneself free.
>
> (Vagnby 2010:22)

No one can take a patent on the concept of festival, and one is free – both researcher and lay person – to present one's own definition. On the basis of the earlier examination and critique of the various points of view, presentations and offerings, I have conceived the following definition, which will serve as one of my tools of analysis in "The Great Festival":

A festival revolves around or cultivates an immaterial activity (artistic experience or expression) that is staged, codified (possibly a ritual or based on a ritual) and programmed. The purpose is to give participants an experience by placing them in a state of self-forgetfulness and engrossment as part of a communal consciousness (*communitas*). The festival lasts four to eight days and is run by a professionally competent leadership. A festival has to have existed for a minimum of 20 years and gone through at least one generation shift.

Dionysian and Apollonian

In western culture, we distinguish between the spiritual and the sensuous. This separation is so sharp that we have named the two human phenomena or conditions after Greek gods, Apollo and Dionysus, who in antiquity's religious universe were the responsible ministers. The Apollonian, with its prudence and limiting moderation, has been carried forth by the Protestant ethic, then further into the Enlightenment with its faith in progress, and ever since the Renaissance it has stood fast in the shifting political, cultural and scientific oriented constructions. The Dionysian is grounded in unbridled boundary crossing, liberation and the uncontrollable. In his article "Self Education and Socialness," Lars Geer Hammershøj (2001) sought to define these two states with the help of Friedrich Nietzsche's "aesthetic figure" in his book *Geburt der Tragödie* (1872):

> This figure can illuminate both transcending of self and the formation of self, which are two features that are more or less significant in different types of education. Thus, the Dionysian can be said to correspond to transcending one's boundaries and the Apollonian to the formation of individuality. And just as education consists of both overshooting and shaping, the Dionysian and Apollonian together form the poles in the Greek tragedy.
>
> The Dionysian is the state of intoxication and unrestrained instincts, and the Dionysian as such, according to Nietzsche, is only understandable as "a surplus of energy." During Dionysian feasts the participants attempted to reach a state of exalted rapture

by imbibing narcotic drinks and through licentious behavior, as well as through dancing and music. The participants strove after a rapturous state that "attempted to obliterate the individual and release it through a mystical feeling of unity" (Nietzsche 1872:30). The Dionysian is intended to transgress individual boundaries and release the self in order to obtain a greater mystical community, where again people are sacredly united.

The Apollonian is just the opposite. The Apollonian state is connected to dreams or the power of the visually evocative. The Apollonian state is seen as both peaceful and contemplative as well as a condition of restraint and restrictions. As a codifying and distinguishing principle, the Apollonian might be said to be the principle of self-individuation:

> For it is the will of Apollo to bring rest and calm to individual beings precisely by drawing boundaries between them, and by reminding them constantly, with this demand for self-knowledge and measure, that these are the most sacred laws in the world.
>
> (Nietzsche 1872:70 (German); Nietzsche 1999:50–51 (English); Hammershøj 2001:28–29)

In this way the controlled individual steps out of his self-acknowledged moderation to occasionally seek out the Dionysian experience at special arrangements – closed: like cultic, religious or club-based parties – or open: like festivals or special forms of dances (Samba, Fado, Hip-hop, Techno).

The dilemma of researching antiquity

When one wants to compare two festivals that occurred with 2000 years between them, one can't avoid treading on two very different research traditions. Even though I chose anthropology, dramaturgy/performance science and experience economy as a common research basis for my analysis.

The Roskilde Festival has naturally been an object of analysis for a succession of sciences from sociology to music science, as well as other cultural and art sciences through to modern experience economy. All of these sciences are both theoretically easily accessible and professionally uncontroversial, understanding that their present theories and fields of practice have been developing through the last 50 years – parallel with the Roskilde Festival's development. Potential contradictions among these sciences are transparent and possible to reconcile or correct, without demanding a redefining of the object. Descriptions and analysis of the Roskilde Festival as such are not split into "schools," unilaterally draped in myth or in-fighting.

The Festival of Dionysus is totally different. In the forms we know it, it ran from about 500 BCE through to the Roman Kaiser Theodosius 1's edict in 391 CE that forbid all heathen forms of culture and activities. Despite the age difference, this festival, without problems, could easily be subjected to the same science that the Roskilde Festival currently enjoys. But for almost two hundred years the Dionysian Feast has been a subject for related areas of study – classic philology and classic archeology – to such a degree that one could say that these research areas have taken a patent on this festival. Through the first half of the 20th century even theater and art historians had to take a back seat as secondary researchers: they were relegated to maintaining the philological and archeological results. The field first opened up to other sciences after the 1950s, resulting in that the other sciences were whirled into antiquity research's growing disputes about interpretation of sources, artifacts and ruins.

A special hurdle was that antiquity researchers supported what one could call "romantic positivism." This archeological and philological tradition is based in romanticism. It unfolds with great authority from there, building on research connected to a large number of excavations in the Mediterranean region. At the same time, democratic ideas were taking hold and being discussed all over Europe and the USA, and were already being implemented constitutionally in several countries. Adding to this, are two streams of thought – one scientific and one ideological – which made a strong impression on scientists, both as researchers and as men, namely positivism and Victorianism.

Romantic idealism was the link between empirical research and morality. The typical antiquity researcher stemmed from the middle or lower trade and manufacturing class, and only after finishing their studies and some modest years as docents could they accede to a professorship and form a family. But these conditions were also sporadic and could in no way – neither economically, socially or morally – compare to the conditions that applied to their objects of study, antiquity's Greek and Roman intellectuals.

Antiquity's colleagues enjoyed the same conditions as (upper class) sportsmen and athletes – they didn't work. Their incomes flowed from their farms or businesses while they lived in city houses. They were served by a large coterie of slaves who fulfilled all their needs – intellectual as well as physical, including preferred sexual needs – ad libitum. In addition to their spouses who insured the generative continuation of the family tree, the Greek intellectual also had (like politicians, top military officers and athletes), an especially well-read or dedicated mistress (hetaera) and/or lover for both intellectual and erotic immersion.

All of this fit poorly into the middle class scientist's concept of family and education. Because of this, a large segment of ancient material was displaced (censured) or converted into something positive. Especially the oppression of antiquity's women in their roles as house wives that we know from the directives, advice and bon mots of Plutarch, Thucydides, Euripides, Sophocles and Herodotus, was idealized as a romantic virtue (Carson 1990:56–57).

Later in the 1800s, when naturalism and positivism had their breakthrough and the romantic female ideal was replaced by male concern connected to pervasive women's liberation (John Stuart Mill's *The Subjection of Women* is from 1869 and Henrik Ibsen's *A Doll's House* from 1879), some antiquity researchers drew support from classic women's oppression, while others were "arguing that things were not as bad for women as they might appear." On the contrary, the first group of antiquity researchers simply believed

> that women deserved everything they got. Understandably a number of scholars have been drawn into Classics by sympathy for the patriarchal character of Greek life, or by a sense of kinship with Greek male homosexuality. . . . Among the visceral misogynists should be counted Friedrich Nietzsche, who began his career as a classical philologist. In his essay "The Greek Woman," he finds it inevitable that an advanced and creative culture should reduce its women to the status of vegetables.
>
> (Keul 1993:9)

As we shall see in the following, to a very high degree, antiquity research was subjected to contemporary overriding aesthetic and political dogma, moral codes, taboos and related morality laws. This led it into many, more or less, self-inflicted fallacies. But luckily, back out again.

Democracy or phallocracy

If today one was to put a label on the constitution that, with the exception of a few oligarch-junta interruptions, applied to the city-state of Athens between 510 and 338 BCE, one would scarcely apply the word "democracy." That the power was in the hands of all the male citizens might possibly lead one to believe that one could compare Athens's constitution with what we know from our own Danish democracy formed in 1849, where voting rights were given to men over 30 (though not servants, welfare recipients, criminal offenders or the insolvent). But this is not completely valid, partly because the Athenian democracy was no parliamentary democracy and partly because their constitution had an entirely different purpose than securing the political rights and influence of male citizens. "Athenian democracy" is more a myth that developed with romanticism during 1900s Europe's formation of democracies with their male voting rights.

The historian Thucydides paraphrased the statesman Pericles's funeral oration for the fallen during the war with Sparta in 430 BCE, in which Pericles mentions some of democracy's side benefits that can be equated with modern democracies:

> Freedom reigns in our public life [*eleuteros*], and if we look at each other's way of daily living, we don't get angry with our neighbor if he lives as he chooses, and we don't bother each other about behavior that isn't legally punishable, but is nevertheless annoying to witness. Privately, we associate without troubling each other, and publicly, fear keeps us from breaking the law.
>
> (Herman Hansen 2005:40)

This has clear parallels to the rights that democracy affords us today. But one can't ignore that this was put forth by politicians who, among other things, held leadership positions for decades, as result of their suggestion to restrict the rights of citizenship to ethnic Athenians. Thus there can be other reasons to praise peace in the private sphere.

Hundreds of years later, Aristotle puts forth precisely the same definition of "freedom":

> The basic principle of democratic constitutions is freedom [*eleutheria*]. It is common perception, and it is based on the idea that freedom exists only under this constitutional form, just as freedom is also claimed as the goal of any democracy. But freedom has two aspects: One is to rule and rule in turn. The other is to live as one pleases, which is said to be a function of freedom. This is true in the same way that the oppressed slave's son is *unable* to live as he pleases.
>
> (Herman Hansen 2005:49)

Being able to *live as one pleases and to enjoy the tranquility of private life* seems to have been the basic freedom requirement in an agreement system, which, of course, also included the most important political rules of behavior as we know them today.

Athenian democracy was thus a deterrent or security system that would prevent the emergence of grueling civil wars between groups or factions of the social and economic upper class, with subsequent empowerment of absolute rulers, or "tyrants." However, it was just as much a system that in part supported and secured the established class and lineage paradigm, and in part retained the form of life that defined the Athenian nobleman and great citizen as imperialist, family chief and man.

This system or paradigm has been called a "Phallocracy." In her book *The Reign of the Phallus* (1993, first published in 1985) Eva C. Keuls defined this constitutional concept in this way:

> phallocracy does not allude to male dominance solely within a private sphere of sexual activity. Instead, as used in this book, the concept denotes a successful claim by a male elite to general power, buttressed by a display of the phallus less as an organ of union or of mutual pleasure than as a kind of weapon: a spear or war club, and a sceptre of sovereignty. In sexual terms, phallocracy takes such forms as rape, disregard of the sexual satisfaction of women, and access to the bodies of prostitutes who are literally enslaved or allowed no other means of support. In the political sphere, it spells imperialism and patriarchal behaviour in civic affairs.
>
> (Keul 1993:2)

The Phallocrat wants to dominate his surroundings, his home, and his city-state. The latter can only happen through vote and competition. But as long as the phallocrat is resigned to this, he can participate in initiating wars, alliances, constructions, and feasts, while at the same time maintaining the life form that constitutes the phallus's regime:

> In the case of a society dominated by men who sequester their wives and daughters, denigrate the female role in reproduction, erect monuments to the male genitalia, have sex with sons of their peers, sponsor public whorehouses, create a mythology of rape, and engage in rampant saber-rattling, it is not inappropriate to refer to a reign of the phallus. Classic Athens was such a society.
>
> (Keul 1993:1)

Phallocracy was not a widespread "form of rule" in Greek city-states. We know, for example, that nurturing/educational practices were very different in Sparta and other city-states, where musical culture was revered (see p. 56 and Comotti 1989:17). Keul also tells us that visitors were not very used to Athenian phallocracy:

> As foreigners were astonished to see, Athenian men habitually displayed their genitals, and their city was studded with statues of gods with phalluses happily erect. The painted pottery of the Athenians, perhaps the most widespread of their arts, portrayed almost every imaginable form of sexual activity.
>
> (Keul 1993:2)

Athenian boys were raised in a phallocracy. The apparent widespread homosexuality was not so much a "tendency" or genetic sexual preference, but rather an integrated part of a phallocratic upbringing:

> Athenian male homosexuality was only one aspect of a larger syndrome which included men's way of relating to boys, wives, courtesans, prostitutes, and other sexual partners.
>
> (Keul 1993:1)

In the phallocratic paradigm the housewife is considered (and protected as) the family's generative resource. It is through her that family genes will be passed on. Her worth is measured exclusively by her paternal ancestry, together with his social and economic position and influence. Her sons will preserve the family genes and her daughters will provide alliances, wealth and connections and preserve the paradigm's greatly valued "bond of blood."

The housewife was "respectable" and had influence on housekeeping and the daughters' upbringing. She was probably a conversational partner for her husband, but didn't garner the same attention or influence as the hetaera, just as she didn't have a veto or access into his homo and/or pedophile séances, or his sexual encounters with the house slaves. The housewife was his companion in official or family contexts and, as mentioned earlier, was portrayed in poetic and historic exhortations as the incarnation of purity, but it was a purity that needed to be protected. This happened through concealment and difficult wedding rituals, where "Putting the lid on female purity was the chief concern and ritual point of the ancient wedding ceremony," a clear example of "masculine clarity and control imposed on a chaos of female promiscuity" (Carson 1990:161).

The housewife's place was first and foremost in the home – according to Plutarch: "The tortoise on which Aphrodite rests her foot symbolizes a woman's life, closed upon itself in its own domestic space," and "neither the body nor the speech of a 'chaste and sensible' woman is 'for the public' " (Carson 1990:156–157). Or Thucydides: "Moreover, her feelings, character and disposition must be kept hidden," while Herodotus in his reference to "the bizarre and reversed world of the Egyptians" with barely disguised disgust also notes: "that these people knead dough with their feet, write from left to right, and send their women out for marketing, while the men stay home and work at the loom" (Carson 1990:157).

Although we know not all noble or burgher housewives tacitly submitted to the phallocratic escapades. If the story about Socrates' wife Xanthippe is to be believed, she not only scolded her husband in full public view for visiting his hetaera, but also dumped his night pan over his head, which, if nothing else, has categorized and immortalized her name.

Women's sexuality was perceived as being explosively boundary crossing and known from "orgies"

> where women in cult-like gatherings (*thiasos*) cultivated the young Dionysus out in open nature in a way that both frightened and fascinated men, who were forbidden to participate. . . . The women, so called man-eaters ("furies"), experienced ecstasy ("to stand outside oneself") and enthusiasm ("when god is inside the human") and in that orgiastic atmosphere they were filled with undreamed of powers and became one with god.
>
> (The Encyclopedia 1994, section under "Dionysus")

The Athenian phallocracy ceased as a democracy in 322 BCE, after the Macedonian occupation force's orders, but continued as a phallocracy as long as the Greek upper class retained the power and economy for it. When Romans later adapted Greek culture into classical Roman education and Athens (Emperor Hadrian) and the Olympic Games (Emperor Nero) were considered cherished places to visit, phallocracy also became a fixed paradigm in the new imperialist world power's constitution (Lund 2005:17ff).

1 In the beginning was the agora

New research

Antiquity research has stormed forward in the last 30 years. Philologists and archeologists, as well as music, culture, art, and performance researchers have all more or less turned earlier perceptions of classical theater and antiquity's music and dance on its head. Contributions to this have come from all over the western world and with such speed that most perceptions of Greek classical theater (and classical Athens) must be considered outdated. Therefore, it is no longer possible in a book like this to refer to available conventional perceptions of technical, artistic, sociological, political, or economic conditions in connection to classical theatrical performances and Dionysian feasts. Today everyone who delves into these subjects must assemble their own impression of the research situation then present their own personal (documented) understanding in dialogue with the many newly minted offerings connected to the ancient Greek festival, its purpose and resources.

This is also what will happen in the following, not just because of interest and sense of duty regarding half a century of intense and engaged research, but also out of necessity. To be able to extract a structural conception of the Athenian Feast of Dionysus that can be compared with other later festivals, there has to be a historically viable and convincing source-based presentation as possible.

The stage is set – and moved

When one visits ancient Greek palaces, theaters, and sports arenas, it quickly becomes apparent that there is always an open area below, in front of, next to, or close by. Today, this space can function as a parking lot or just as an open flat area. But it is there, and it functioned clearly as an *agora* – a square, marketplace, meeting, or festival space (see Figure 1.1).

In Argos, it sits as a ruin below the palace, just a little bit away from the theater. In Epidaurus, it sits in front of the large theater opposite the medical/health center. The little Epidaurus theater also has an open area in front of the entrance. Below the palace in Mycenae, there is also a large square.

The agora has been the central area since the first urban society, and we still see its ruins in classical settlements. Corinth presents the clearest example, with its quite large agora and remains of shops built into the walls around the square that also included a large tribune or speaker's podium (rostra). Above the agora and next to the medical/health center is the Apollonian temple – and a few hundred meters from there, the theater.

There has also been a tradition for researchers to put emphasis on the theater's religious function and affiliation, yes, going as far as

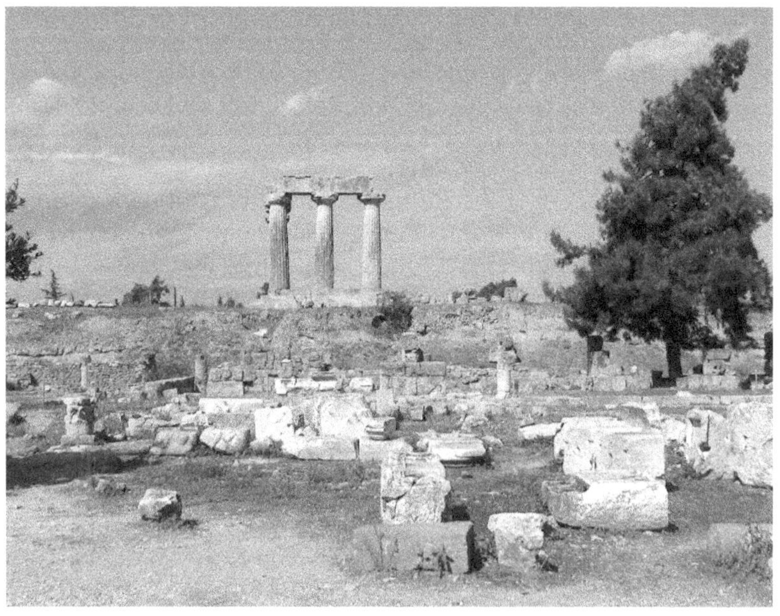

A

Figure 1.1 The Agora in Corinth with Apollonian temple, shops, and speaker's podium

Source: Author's photo

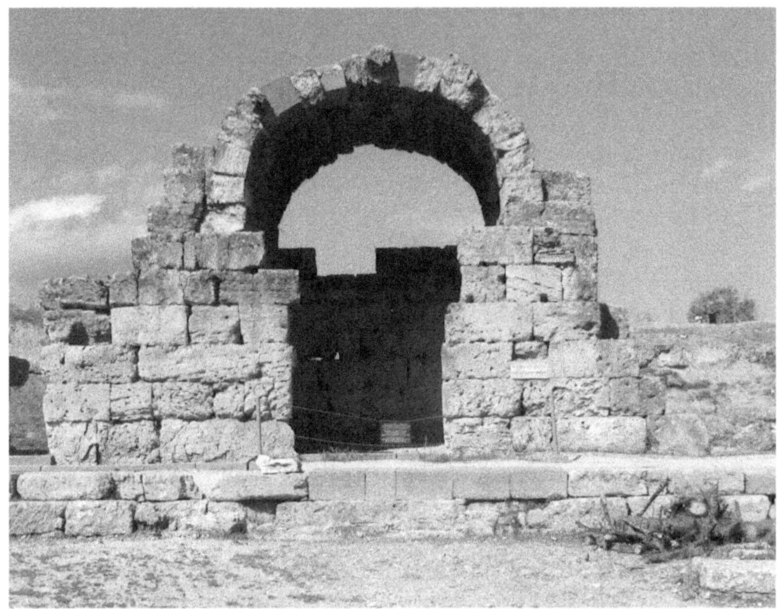

B

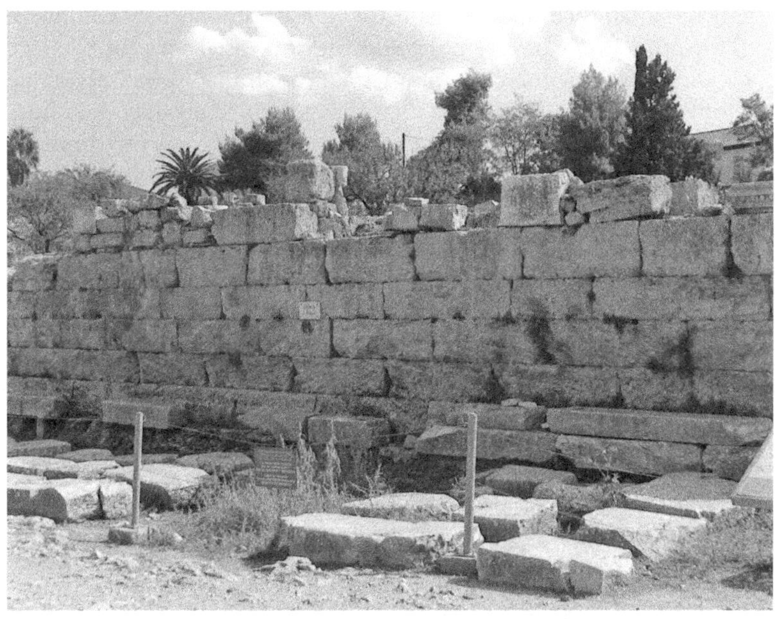

C

Figure 1.1 Continued

Source: Author's photo

to consider the theater itself as monumental religious architecture. According to Rune Frederiksen this perception is based

> primarily on the Athenian evidence. Here the dramatic activities were connected with the worship of Dionysos during various festivals in which *ta dionysia ta en astei* [the Dionysian festival in the city] took place in the theatre located in the *temenos* (holy area/shrine) of Dionysos Eleutherios. However, Athens and a few other major *poleis* had separate buildings for political meetings of the people – which was quite uncommon – and a religious function and significance of theatres in such *poleis* may, accordingly more easily be identified or, at least postulated. . . .
>
> From one point of view the theatres from the rest of the Greece can be interpreted like the theatre in Athens: they are all equipped with scene buildings, which unambiguously indicates the building's use for dramatic activities and proves that the theatres were constructed (or rebuilt) as centres for dramatic festivals. That, of course, strongly supports the interpretation of the theatre as a religious building in general terms; but in a study like the present we cannot stop here: (1) the presence of a scene building is not at all incompatible with the well-attested use of the theatre for other types of assembly; and they may well have been more 'important' for the community than the dramatic festivals which only occupied the theatre a few days a year. They may even have been so important that it was the political, and not the dramatic activities, which, at some localities, had been the reason for the erection of the theatre, (2) furthermore: it is clear that the scene building was used for *performance;* But does that performance necessarily have to be dramatic and linked to Dionysos, and therefore religious?
>
> (Frederiksen 2000:81)

The theater was a political, communications and entertainment facility tied to the city or the center's actual function: defense (Mycenae, Argos, Sparta, Athens), healing (Epidaurus, Corinth), trade (Corinth, Athens), political advising and/or sports competitions (Delphi, Epidaurus) and festivals (Athens) (see Figures 1.2–1.5).

The theater was never located in the center of the buildings, and was always subordinate to the palace, the square, the sports arena, and the medical/health center. The agora was both central and multi-functional. Two modern supermarket theorists, Helen

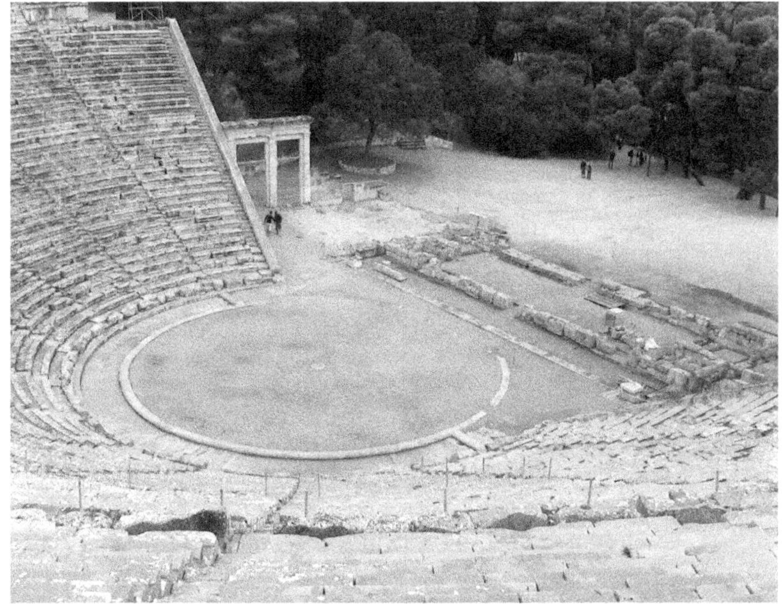

Figure 1.2 The theater in Epidaurus

Source: Author's photo

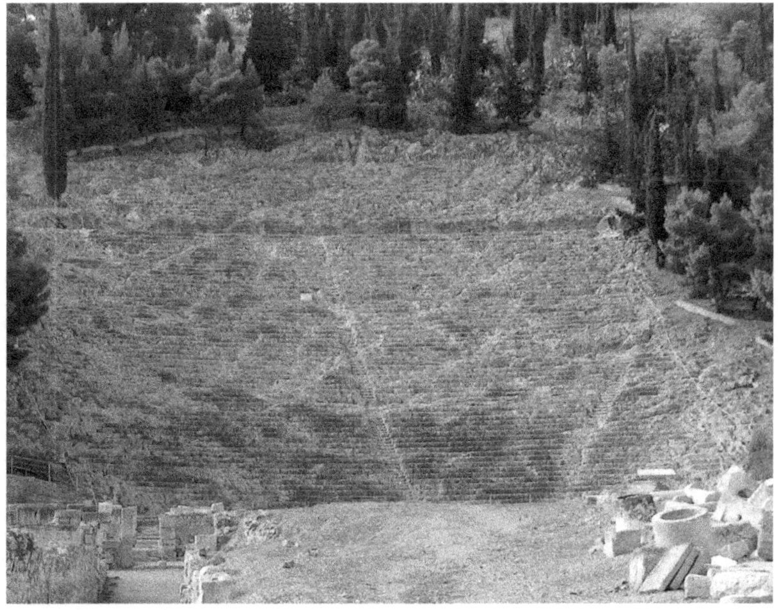

Figure 1.3 The theater in Argos

Source: Author's photo

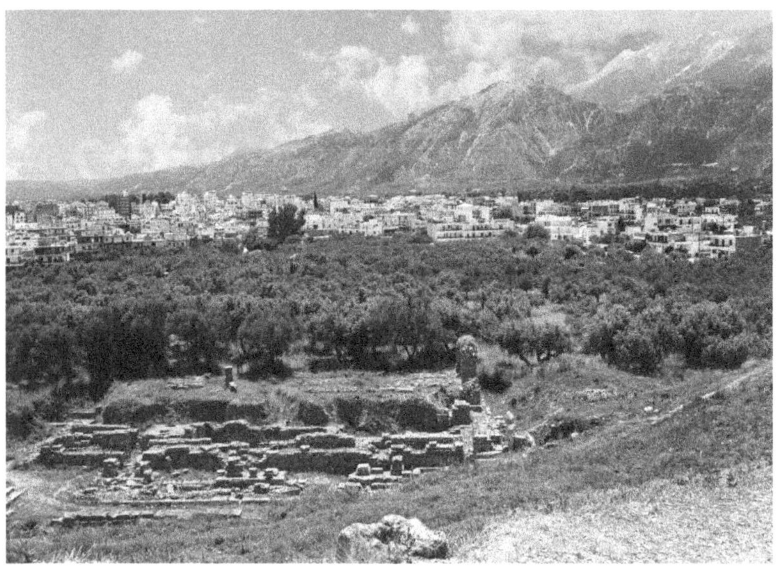

Figure 1.4 The theater in Sparta

Source: Wikimedia Commons

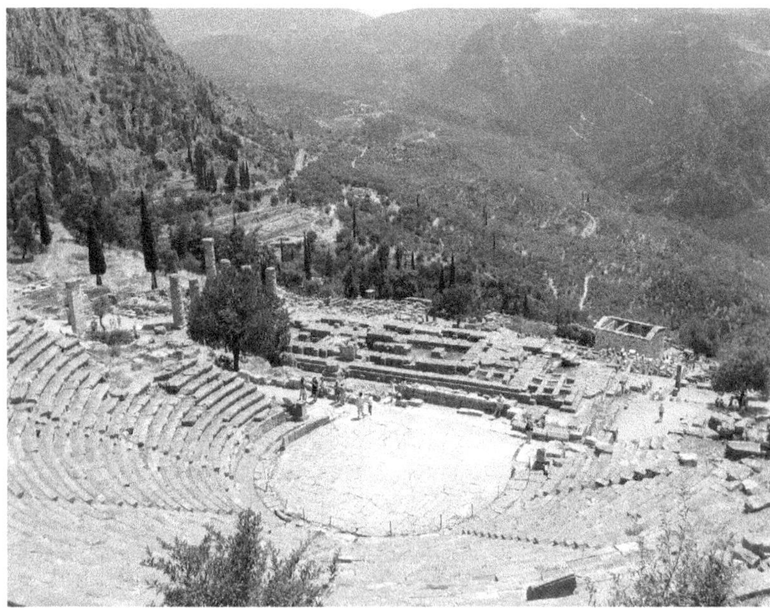

Figure 1.5 The theater in Delphi

Source: Wikimedia Commons

Tangires and Peter Coleman give this definition of the classic market place:

> A large open square reserved for all public functions. The civic center, or **agora** as it was known in the ancient Greek world, served as the site not only for trade and commerce but also for administration, legislative, judicial, social and religious activities. The location of markets in the agora was convenient for city dwellers, vendors bringing goods by road or water and officials responsible for overseeing the markets.
>
> (Tangires 2008:9)

> For the Greeks, trading took place in the *agora*. This was an open square formed as a meeting-place, often between the ruling palace and the town's principal buildings, and was intermittently used as a market. On market days, goods were laid out on mats or on temporary stalls to allow other activities – such as voting and debate, public displays, sports and parades – to take place outside market days. The earliest trading took place at the hub of the settlement, and so established the integrated relationship between trading and the heart of civilized activity in the centre of towns.
>
> (Coleman 2006:19)

As mentioned, we see the remains of this disposition in Athens as the agora seems to have been moved a little around the Acropolis hill. It is interesting that the theater, as an institution, is not discussed by Tangires and Coleman, but of course is contained in the categories "social and religious activities" and "public displays, sports and parades." This is the correct assumption for the theater that we know today as "The Greek Theater." David Wiles formulates in this manner:

> It is a commonplace of theatre history that Greek drama began in the Agora, the marketplace of Athens. A dictionary compiled from unknown sources explains the Greek word for "bleachers" with reference to the wooden seats in the agora "from which they used to watch the Dionysian contests before the theatre in the sanctuary of Dionysus was built," and relates the word "orchestra" [the stage] to a dancing place in the agora. . . . It is now known that the "archaic" agora was sited on the north-east slope of the Acropolis, site of the modern Plaka, and it was probably here and

> not in the flat classical agora [on the north side] that comedy and tragedy began.
>
> (Wiles 2003:96)

But during the course of the first half of the 400s BCE several of the agora's functions were divided – and moved. The tradespeople probably felt bothered by the many artistic, political and sports related activities, just as a more prestigious presentation of these functions were very much on the city-state's leaders' minds. For David Wiles it's not just a question of a practical solution:

> A new space for dancing and drama was hollowed out on the south slope of the Acropolis, another for political assemblies on a nearby hill called the Pnyx; the level classical agora [which was erected below the north slope] was a space for processions, courts and rites around altars, but not for large-scale drama. This fragmentation of civic space had long-term consequences for western culture.
>
> (Wiles 2003:96–97)

And with a not to be misinterpreted graphic Wiles shows how the archaic agora "the civic hearth," is broken up into a trade and administrative agora, a public gathering platform, as well as a playhouse *in* or just *with* Dionysus' name (Dahl 2010:38). But even though the new, large trade agora could still make room for parades, as well as judicial and religious rituals (with a view to the obligatory Apollonian temple, erected on the closest hill), the theater was relegated to the opposite slope where it soon had a concert hall and a hospital for neighbors.

David Wiles doesn't seem to be convinced of the existence of a round dance area (orchestra) in the agora, and with the separation of the theater from trade activities, it would come to form the stage for the newly constructed theater. His doubt is supported by the archeologist Elisabeth Gebhard's pointing out the existence of rectangular and trapezoidal theaters in the 5th century BCE. (Dahl 2010:80, more about this on pp. 27–28). Just as it is suggested that theater performances were staged on the agora on erected and easily dismountable wooden tribunes. (Pickard-Cambridge 1946:11–13) Under all circumstances the Athenian separation of the theater from the agora became a standard Greek practice, notes Wiles, who adds:

> But there seemed no long-term logic in separating the functions of theatre and political arena. Advances in acoustical design

> meant that a dancing place and a speaking place could conveniently be one of the same, so theatres doubled as places of assembly. Drama was framed by Greek culture as an ethico-political activity, located outside the space of purchase, consumption and daily social intercourse.
>
> (Wiles 2003:97)

In this way the theater was something one would "go to" – literally: out of the market area and over to the theater. That is to say, out of the public arena and into the art of the theater. Though this didn't mean that the theater as an idea immediately left the market space. The American sociologist Richard Sennett formulates it like this: "The classical ideal of the *theatrum mundi* attempted to convey one union of aesthetics and social reality. Society is a theatre, and all men are actors" (Sennett 1976:313). And he cites Nicolas Evreinoff (*The Theatre in Life* 1927) for this definition of world theater:

> Examine any . . . branch of human activity and you . . . will see that kings, statesmen, politicians, warriors, bankers, business men, priests, doctors, all pay daily tributes to theatricality, all comply with the principles ruling on the stage.
>
> (Sennett 1976:313)

But did the market square thus, for a thousand years before the theater's relocation, constitute what Richard Sennett calls a space for "The Public Man?" Did the Athenian Agora continue to play this role for a few more centuries? After which it jumps to the Forum Romanum then continues, after Emperor Augustus, in various dilutions up through the Middle Ages, only to end with the *The Fall of Public Man* (the title of Sennett's 1976:3 book)

It has always been antiquity historians' great pleasure to present this ideal image of the theatrical agora, where the great spirits, "the public men," completely dominated the communal sphere (Mejer 1994:149–150). And it is correct that the market and festival square, for two thousand years all the way up to the present, again and again, managed to create that resonant and open space that for all time would institute "the public man" and also today "the public woman."

2 The Dionysian feast

The festival square: hall and tribune

Today the word "theater" can refer to the theater building, the stage, the audience area, the play, the production, the performance, or the drama. In the conventional use of the word, the audience sits in a theater space and looks up or down at the stage. The theater or building is divided into the hall and the stage. In front of the stage there can be a foyer and behind the stage a backstage. Theater has (still following the conventional view) existed since the ancient Greeks who, through several hundred years, approximately 500–200 BCE, developed it into the perfect "amphitheater", which today we can see more or less well preserved remains of in Turkey, Greece and southern Italy. Ever since this period, both architecturally and artistically, this has become the norm for all theaters.

The problem for the modern theater or concert-goer is, of course, that the original designations for the theatrical structure's individual parts no longer are meaningful: The original stage is rightfully or wrongfully called the "orchestra" – which means dancing area. The rows of benches that were set up around this or the seating area that was established up a slope, was called the *teatron* or the place for spectators: The area where the public can watch what is happening on the orchestra. Immediately behind the orchestra and directly opposite the teatron a wooden wall was erected, that both served as a scenographic backdrop for the play that is taking place on the orchestra and a dividing wall, behind which the performers could change masks and costumes. Eventually, as theaters grew larger, one built them from stone, and with a covered platform in front of the stage wall – the proscenium, or the downstage – from which the performers could better be seen and heard (Hjortsø 1968:68–70, Isager 1985:14).

None of these old Greek designations corresponds directly to our era. Today we use the term "orchestra" as a designation for those seats that are closest to the stage. The proscenium and downstage are the most forward part of the stage and the theater (teatron) designates, as already mentioned, the entire building – the stage, the public seating tribune, as well as the foyer and the backstage.

Despite their precise and inviolable definitions of the theater's structural elements, archeologists, philologists, antiquity historians and theater historians, have a certain responsibility for this terminological confusion. The genesis of the Greek theater is described by most researchers (Blume 1978:47) as a direct development of the rural village's original threshing ground. Its function as a festival and dancing area, according to the common view, became the orchestra (stage), which then evolved into a spectator area (teatron), the stage, (the backstage wall) and the proscenium (downstage). After this, from the years 5–400 BCE, full Greek theater structures were erected (admittedly with stage, backstage wall and spectator benches made of wood), where hundreds of tragedies and comedies were performed. From the 32 tragedies, 11 comedies, and 2 satyr plays that are preserved (Isager 1985:23, Thomsen 1985:40), with the help of Aristotle (Due 1985:23, Blume 1978:2), Plato and other later authors' analysis and accounts, researchers have attempted to reconstruct Greek theater's techniques and production conditions, religious and societal functions, plays' dramaturgy and impact, as well as the audience's composition and reactions. Several of the mentioned researchers (especially Bodil Due) are aware of the problem of reconstructing theater from 5–400 BCE from the vague 300 BCE texts of Aristotle. But all are agreed on the goal: to canonize the surviving Athenian 400 BCE's tragedies in form, content and significance:

> And this art form was created in an unimpressive spot, a little city with 30–40,000 residents, and was shown just a few times a year, and in an arena that wasn't larger than a schoolyard. To this day, we are seized by the greatness and passion of the Greek tragedy.
> (Hjortsø 1968:65).

The wooden Greek theater

Theaters made from stone that we today see all around southern Europe and Asia Minor are all over a hundred or several hundred years younger than the wooden theaters where Greek tragedies, comedies and satyr plays were first performed. Just as *Hamlet* didn't endure the anguish of existentialism in the contemporary Kronborg castle in Denmark, *Medea, Antigone, Oedipus* and *Agamemnon*, first set their clogs on the marble Dionysian stage 150–175 years after the plays' geneses – long after they had become repertoire theater with much else besides the classics on the program.

In educational literature as well as in tourist lectures there is a tradition for rather vigorous re-design. Discussions of the dramatists Aeschylus, Sophocles, Euripides and Aristophanes and their plays are always illustrated with photos of far younger stone theaters, and preferably in the best preserved theater in Epidaurus from circa 300 BCE which was largely remodeled and expanded at the start of the 100s BCE (Erbe 1962:17, Hjortsø 1968:70–71). These discussions are never illustrated with drawn reconstructions of the wooden theaters with their stage sheds and rows of wooden spectator benches. The explanation is that theater architecture's great epoch was from 330 BCE and onward, a 100 years after Athens's building, sculpture, poetic dramas, democracy, politics, and military glory in 400 BCE. These buildings were therefore not built for the classic tragedies and comedies that we know today, but for revisions of them and for new forms of theater, dance and music entertainment as well as gladiator competitions that were oriented toward the larger public and international potentates and their guests. And theaters remained like this and served this purpose all the way up to the Roman emperors' embrace of Christianity as the state religion in the beginning of the 300s BCE. These theaters were also used for Dionysian feasts in both cities and in countryside and for sports competitions in Olympia, Delphi, Sparta, Epidaurus, and Athens and many other places in the Roman provinces.

Theater entertainment had become popular – so popular that the Athenian assembly in 300 BCE granted citizens free entrance (Isager 1985:10), which probably only meant that the state didn't exactly need this yearly income, as opposed to the owners of earlier epochs' bleacher scaffolding (see Figure 2.1). At the same time, the theater was a political instrument in the popular assembly's hands. The greater public, in Athens up to 17,000 and in Epidaurus 15,000, put forth growing demands regarding technical refinement – rotating decorations, wagons for set pieces, and cranes that could bring actors swaying or flying onto the stage. Also the acoustics had to be improved, partly by using funneled megaphone amplifiers in the actors' masks. And in respect to the audience sitting in the back rows, the actors gave up the classical performances' soft and malleable footwear and now toddled around with stiff thick soles beneath their boots (Erbe 1962:16–17).

The modest 400s BCE theater, with wooden benches on a fragile scaffolding around a dance area and with a minimal boarded partition as backdrop, culminated with the Dionysian feast's drama competition of 458 BCE when the wooden bleachers collapsed during the performance of Aeschylus's tragedy *Agamemnon* – or maybe it was his

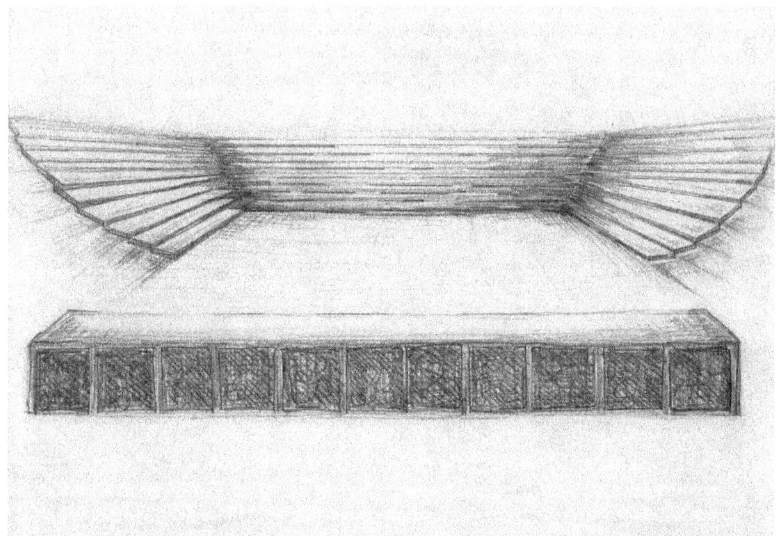

Figure 2.1 Drawing of the basic Dionysian wooden theater, as it might have looked during Sophocles and Euripides's time (by Jo Juncker Harsløf, based on a model by Christian Schieckel, The German Theater Museum, Munich)
Source: Reproduced from Dahl 2010:87

subsequent more juicy satyr play that set the fatal wooden structure swaying? This event gave the Athenian city council reason to consider a more solid structure for the spectators (Vitruvius 1955:ix): most immediately, as a partially stabilized rectangular wooden structure on a stone block foundation (Dahl 2010:87, see Figure 2.2). It was more than a hundred years later that they erected the architectural and professionally engineered theater made from marble and stone that we know from calendars, lecture tours, and educational materials.

It was first around 330 BCE, under Athens's financial officer Lycurgus, that the extensive renovations took place that we see the remains of today.

Repertoire

The myth of the 400s BCE arena being built from white marble is just as ineradicable as that of the stage's development from threshing ground to fully developed Dionysus Theater, or the performance's

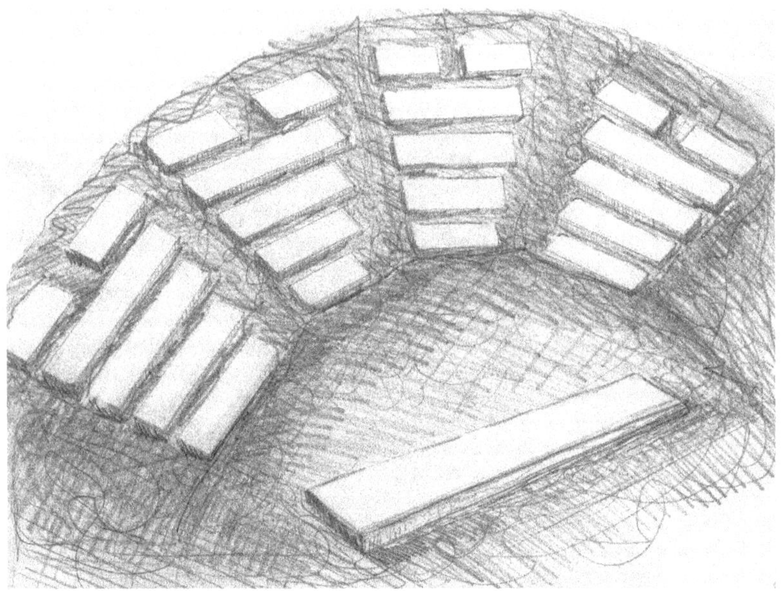

Figure 2.2 Drawing of the Dionysus Theater in 430 BCE with a trapezoidal shaped orchestra by Jo Juncker Harsløf

development from Dionysian dance to glorious tragedy. In the mythomaniac's optic the annual three days of tragic plays becomes the highpoint of the theater facility's function. This latter misconception, however, can only be sustained by the repression of the theater's overall artistic, political, and social purposes.

The buildings' facilities were fully utilized, as we have seen with Rune Frederiksen (2000:81) and David Wiles (2003:96–97), for those functions that they were constructed for: concerts, dances, satyr plays and comedies, entertainment and business meetings. On the orchestra (the dance area) dances continued to be performed (always accompanied by music). From the orchestra – where the acoustics were optimal – concerts and tragedies were also presented. Some of the theater pieces were performed from the proscenium, accompanied by music on the orchestra, where eventually inserted dances were also developed. Comedies and farces were performed from the orchestra.

One has to imagine that the Dionysus Theater in Athens presented a year round repertoire of dance and music performances, interrupted by two larger festivals (the Lenaia Festival in January and the Dionysus Festival in March) with races, sports, dances, music and poetry contests, where also the dramatists, actors and theater producers competed for first prizes. After the 4th century BCE public interest for tragedies waned, while especially comedies and comedy-like entertainments were winning a growing popularity (Green 1994:1). Together with music and dance programs, they all demanded more technically from the theater facility, which was continuously expanded and refined.

The playwrights

Who were these playwrights then? We've been handed down tragedies and satyr plays written by three dramatists, and comedies written by one. Of the three tragedians we know that Aeschylus (circa 525–456 BCE) was the son of a landowner and partook as an officer in the Persian Wars, both in the battle of Marathon and at the defeat of the Persian fleet at Salamis in 480 BCE (Dugdale 2008:158, The Encyclopedia 1994). In contrast to Aeschylus' extensive production of theater plays (approximately 80), his accomplishments at Marathon were mentioned on his gravestone (Dugdale 2008:159). Sophocles, the son of a weapon maker, was also an officer/general (circa 495–406 BCE, during the Samian War). As a member of the political "jet set" (Dugdale 2008:164, Green 1994:13) Sophocles was an active member of The Delian League's (a maritime alliance) 10 man college, a war strategist, and a colleague of Pericles, approximately 441 BCE, and reappointed 428 BCE, the year after Pericles's death. Sophocles was also a member of the crisis committee during the second Peloponnesian War (415–404 BCE) after the defeat at Syracuse in 415 BCE. In addition to this, Sophocles secured a priesthood with the Asclepius Cult (Pauly 1996, Dugdale 2008:164), which maybe was just a biography-friendly rebranding of "epidemic commissioner," who assisted with the health catastrophe, including the establishment of the Asclepius Hospital, treating the many victims of the plague in the tightly populated Athens in 429 BCE, as well during the Spartan siege in the following year. Sophocles's production of approximately 120 tragedies and satyr plays, in this context, must be considered almost as a dramatic hobby.

Aeschylus and Euripides (485–406 BCE) both had aristocratic backgrounds, while Sophocles's position in society was tempered by belonging to the manufacturing or trade bourgeoisie (Dugdale 2008:163, Hauser 1989:74). Aeschylus and Euripides supported themselves with their farms or businesses as well as their military and political offices. Neither of them would have been able to make a living from the occasional prizes they received when they won drama competitions. Their dramatic occupations were, like the hundreds of others participating in the 400s BCE competitions, done in their spare time and as amateur dramatists. Aristophanes's (circa 450–386 BCE) ancestry and social connections are not known, but he also garnered a political-administrative position for a period, as a prytan for his fyle (district representative in the popular assembly), and Arnold Hauser places him (together with Aeschylus and Sophocles) "on the side of aristocracy and reaction" (Pauly 1989, Hauser 1989:74). Euripides and Aristophanes, who we know the least about, might well have made a professional livelihood from their theater, music and dance productions through sales and performances at other Attic or Peloponnesian venues. Euripides himself also seems to have participated in several of his own pieces and theater plays (Erbe 1962:16, Green 1994:13).

Women in the theater?

For the last hundred years, antiquity and theater researchers have discussed whether or not it was only free men who had access to the theater. The assumption that women were forbidden to attend performances was based on text analysis of tragedies and comedies, in combination with the certain knowledge that all roles were acted by men and boys. Several researchers (Friis Johansen 1985:17, Isager 1985:11–12) also note that it isn't apparent from the preserved comedies (of Aristophanes) nor any actual legal documentation that women, children and slaves shouldn't have had access to theater performances.

The question itself is clearly formulated from a conventional 1800s positivistic male point of view. Holger Friis Johansen points to a couple of references to this by Plato and states: "that tragedies in his [Plato's] time were attended by men and women and children, and possibly also slaves: and we have no reliable source telling us that the makeup of the audience changed about or shortly after the year 400" (Friis Johansen 1985:17).

Or how is one to understand the following quote from Bodil Due other than to assume there was open entrance for women from the child bearing age on up: Aeschylus (dramatist, director, stage designer etc.) became very famous for his "masks and costumes for the chorus in *Eumenides.* The chorus consisted of the goddesses of revenge, Erinys, and when they first come on stage their appearance was supposed be so frightening that it scared the wits out of spectators and caused women to abort on the spot" (Bodil Due 1985:29).

Live Hov however points out that "it's uncertain if this source actually reflects the circumstances in Aeschylus's own time," and thinks that "this anecdote" about fainting children and aborting women is accepted too uncritically (Hov 1998:128).

Herbert William Parke also mentions this Eumenides example as one of several indications that women were sitting in the audience and adds:

> Also Aristophanes's humorous picture of the women of Athens as enraged against Euripides because of his presentation of their sex in his plays is much more plausible and effective if they could actually have seen these tragedies. To suppose that they simply knew of them from male gossip or from rare facility of written texts would have been much less convincing. On the other hand there are several passages in Aristophanes' comedies which seem to enumerate the age groups of the audience only in terms of males or otherwise imply that no women are in the theatre.
>
> (Parke 1977:130)

Though he doesn't present any of the "passages" but is content to refer to older discussions about this question, Jørgen Mejer isn't in doubt for a moment. He states: "While there were only men and boys performing, it looks like there were both men and women, citizens and foreigners as well as slaves that could watch the performances" (Mejer 1994:154)

One of the most recent proposals comes from the American Eric Dugdale, who in a piece about audiences writes: "Whether women were also present is a question that is still debated, though there is increasing consensus that they did, if in smaller numbers and perhaps at the margins" (Dugdale 2008:133).

Christian Dahl positions himself squarely in Dugdale's corner and repeats the often cited Plato quote where it specifically says: "that women, among them respectable housewives, were present in the audience," but also adds: "This strains against an otherwise unreasonable assumption that at least socially well-positioned women stayed away from the theater just as they did other public presentations" (Dahl 2010:48). But this conclusion doesn't pass the "phallocracy test." The theater with its audience of state officials, distinguished guests, aristocrats, and citizens is exactly the kind of public circumstance where the housewife could appear with her husband and her husband hardly would be without her. Remember that she had nothing else but her respectability albeit in the expanded sense of provocative opinions and the courage of her actions. It was precisely this that the tragedies were about. She could recognize and completely identify with the tragic female figures – Medea, Antigone, Jocasta, Clytemnestra. Without this strongly focused core audience of proud and suffering cohorts among the spectators, the performances would be completely without the direction and meaning that all theater and performance has and has had.

But the housewife was also a necessity at comedy performances both as an alibi for her husband and as a defender of her own respectability. Aristophanes's comedy *Lysistrata* is a good example of this. The piece purports to show that married women, by denying the marriage bed to their husbands, could force them to stop the war. But everyone in the audience knew that this same bed existed primarily for generative reasons and that the lord of the manor had his hetaera, his slaves, his bordello and his young men and boys to release the night and day's erotic pressures. The piece is a conservative tribute to the idea of the respectable wife who here, in the comedy's amusing fiction, is also the husband's lover almost as if she was his hetaera!

Phallocracy's fundamental law number one demanded respect for the legitimately married woman in reality as well as in fiction, in tragedy as well as in comedy.

This question of a woman's access to the theater, as mentioned earlier, was originally posed in a time when theater censorship was exercised by the national Justice Minister, and was inescapable throughout the western world, where all moral and erotic indecencies, under Victorian conventions, were banned from theatrical stages (Skafte Jensen 2004:150, with reference to Pickard-Cambridge 1953). What self-respecting 1800s positivistic researcher would take his wife or daughter to a genuine Greek performance of Aristophanes's *Lysistrata* or a juicy satyr play with its costumes and impressive attribute amplifications, the same amplifications that appear so clearly on frescoes, ceramic jars and sculptures hidden away in cellars of Archeological Museums all over Europe?

In her book *Kvinnerollene i antikkens teater – skrevet, spilt og sett av menn* (1998) (*Women's Role in Antiquity's Theater – Written, Performed and Seen by Men*), which is the most in-depth examination of the question of women in antiquity's theater, Live Hov agrees with the point of view that women had access to the festivals' performances, comedies as well as tragedies. Though she thinks that one can still discuss what portion of the total audience they made up, did they sit in separate areas from the men (and did the hetaera sit separately from the rest of the women) and were they relegated to the worst seats in the theater?

However, Live Hov elevates this question to a higher level. Taking her starting point from Synnøve des Bouvrie's division of a "dramatic," a "symbolic'" and a "tragic" level of analysis, she asserts that the dramatic level is absolutely the most interesting in this context:

> It is here that we find the roles' concrete material, even the word-sound of the dialogue that in the drama's own time and in later times were performed on the theater's stage. It was this dialogue that reached the audience's ears with statements about a women's duty and a women's nature, as a statement of a female figure's thoughts and reactions.
>
> (Hov 1998:136)

My conclusion regarding the question of "women's presence in ancient Greek theater?" In context of performance practices, precisely these kind of negative characteristics for women could be perceived as a dramaturgically effective means to maintain a large, mixed audience of men and women, young and old.

Music and song

A recurring problem for both antiquity and theater historians is that the tragedies, comedies and satyr plays incontrovertible musical accompaniment has not been accessible in ways other than the visual (frescoes, reliefs, vases etc.) and textual (directly mentioned and commented on in the pieces themselves, or in preserved descriptions by contemporary spectators). Most historians thus chose to only briefly mention that the instrumental aspect was there, for example, as a characteristic of the actor's voice:

> He was an interpreter of the word, a declaimer. The play gave him his voice and his character; his voice doesn't need to be forced; it clearly comes through thanks to the Greek theater's magnificent natural space, but the voice was supported by music, lyre or flute.
>
> (Hjortsø 1968:72)

Regarding the unnecessary forcing of the voice, this applies only to standard theaters. In Athens and Epidaurus's theaters, where the spectator seating was expanded by 5,000–10,000 places in the 300s and again in the 100s BCE, the voices could no longer reach the back rows without amplification.

Theater music was no longer just supportive accompaniment but it was completely integrated into the performances:

> Music was an important component of Greek tragedy, and both Aeschylus and Sophocles composed their music themselves. Euripides did this as well and when, after a visit to Macedonia, he was inspired to explore new musical ideas, it gave him an opportunity for gross parodies, for example in Aristophanes' "The Frogs." One of Euripides' innovations was an art *monody*, a kind of dance aria designed to be performed by one of the actors. One has an example of this in "Orestes." Euripides also introduced an echoed lament as something new. This can be found in the parody of Aristophanes in "Thesmophoriazusai [The Festival of Thesmophoria]."
>
> (Erbe 1962:17)

Other theater historians have had more difficulty reconciling themselves to the lack of audio or musically notated documentation of classic Greek theater music. Horst-Dieter Blume formulates it like this:

> Greek drama in the classical period forms a complex picture: the spoken word, music and dance formed a unit that we can't precisely recreate because tradition has only preserved the first of the above named three elements. Aeschylus was famous for creating numerous new dance forms for his choir, and the choreography was probably geared toward a danceable mimesis that helped clarify the plot. Euripides, on the other hand, enjoyed a special reputation as a composer; we hear that his songs and arias were on everyone's lips. This kind of information puts us in the position to measure the scope of this loss; we have little to go on with the reduction to pure text; without the danceable and the musical, a precise historical reproduction cannot be achieved.
>
> (Blume 1978:2)

All three tragedy dramatists were also composers, just as they all both directed and acted now and then in the performances. In addition to this, Aeschylus was also a choreographer. Today this kind of multi-talent would hardly be called a dramatist, but rather a performance artist. Their clearly documented composing and choreographic skills have not led to the mentioning of any of them in modern discussions of dance and musical history.

In addition to this, regarding the music, one might expect that music researchers would long ago have tried to reconstruct antiquity's rhythms, styles – and yes, even the melodies, if for no other reason, but for the benefit of theater historians. But this only first started to happen in recent decades, in conjunction with the growing interest in "third world music" or "world music."

"The singing jar"

For more than one hundred years, archeologists and art historians have maintained that antiquity's sculptures, reliefs, friezes and temples, also in their own epochs, appeared as white marble. They asserted this, despite the emergence of photo technology (ultraviolet photography) in the 1960s and again even later, when finely tuned technology in the 1980s became available to the humanities and modern conservation science and could bring forth the color that was part of the finished work of art, also in its own era (Østergaard 2009).

To this very day, we still can't, in any way, play back the ceramic jars, trays and reliefs that are decorated with musicians and dancers so that we might hear the music or see the dances. While we wait for technology, we of course can't repeat the romantic era's pale copies of sculptures and statues or theater historian's reconstructions of theaters from dramatic texts alone. Let us instead look more closely at antiquity's instruments, rhythms, scales, musical notations, and acoustic possibilities.

The music culture

Our knowledge of antiquity's music is quite extensive and established, based as it is on the works of a number of musically knowledgeable Greek scholars:

> Reliable evidence regarding the origin of Greek music is preserved by the author of the dialogue *De Musica,* attributed to Plutarch. It is particularly a valuable source because it is based on the works of Pythagorean, Academic, and Peripatetic scholars, such as Glaucus of Rhegium, Heraclides Ponticus, and Aristoxenus, who were well informed about the musical culture of archaic Greece [ca. 625–480].
>
> (Comotti 1989:13)

Therefore, there was a strong and developed musical culture that, toward the end of the 6th century BCE, encountered steadily growing festival and theater competitions. Music, like dance, was ready to facilitate chorus and theater forms that were still just in their infancy:

> The development of intense poetic and musical activity after the end of the Mycenean age [circa 1100 BCE] is connected with the profound change which Greek society underwent just at this time. . . . The relationship between town and country ceased to be one of sheer contrast, as it had been earlier when the king from his fortified citadel subjected the surrounding countryside to his rule. The two became integrated, with the fringes of the newly established *polis*, the city-state, coinciding with the regional borders in a pattern of territorial organization that had no precedent in the ancient world.
>
> The new political structure gave citizens increasing opportunities for participating in the different forms of community life: religious festivals, ceremonies of the *thiasoi* (associations of the initiated in the cults of certain gods), and banquets of the *hetaerae* (for those belonging to one or another political faction). Public festivals included as a rule the performance of choral composition, according to their purpose. . . . symposia also provided the occasion for exchanges of ideas, for political debates, and for programs of action. Music and song not only contributed to making this communal experience more pleasurable but often became the instruments of political and cultural propaganda.
>
> (Comotti 1989:14–15)

Originally, each region had its own repertoire that was passed on from generation to generation. But eventually the most known melodies spread and generated fixed forms of melodic structure, which was used across large swaths of Greece. In the 670s BCE Terpander, a musician from Lesbos, opened a conservatory in Sparta and won first prize in the music competition that took place during the 26th Olympiad in 676–673 BCE (Comotti 1989:16). A few years later Taletas from Gortina opened yet another conservatory in Sparta.

In the seventh century, then, Sparta was the most important musical center of Greece. Music and gymnastics formed the basis of education for boys and girls, who after seven years of age, were schooled in common by the state. Choral song was meant to fulfill a paideutic function with regard to the community as a whole because it reinforced essential values of public morality, such as love for the fatherland and respect for the law. In this cultural environment, musicians from all of

Greece made considerable contributions to the repertory of Spartan songs. (Comotti 1989:18)

In the 7th and 6th centuries BCE, conservatories spread all over Greece, on the mainland as well as on the islands. Aside from Sparta, Lesbos was also a musical center, with the poets and singer/composers Alcaeus and Sappho as major innovative producers. But the proliferation of conservatories and musical milieus extended to the outer colonies in southern Italy and to the city-states in Sicily (Comotti 1989:19–21).

Thus, through the 6th century BCE, music culture seems to have constituted the largest cohesive cultural and musical force in the Greek speaking world. It bound all of the rituals, political events, communications, sports, entertainment (festivals) and erotic forms together. At the same time, with its innumerable music schools and teachers, music culture could boast of a much larger theoretical foundation than other contemporary art forms (poetry, storytelling, architecture, visual art, theater).

Just a few antiquity researchers have paid attention to music's paramount social significance. For a majority, music was just an accompaniment to or "included as an important part of community life" (The Encyclopedia 1994:Ancient Greece). But music was not just "included as an important part of community life," it was ubiquitous – in society's physical, logistic, artistic, ritualistic, pedagogic and collective consciousness.

Sparta established its military strength in the conservatories, but also initially developed it in its musical education where the schooling was not separated by gender. In the 5th century BCE, Athens the importance of music in education seemed to be aimed more toward children and young people's spiritual development. One of Athens's greatest cultural personalities was the music theorist and pedagogue Damon, who was the leading statesman Pericles's teacher and advisor. Damon put forth the following musical consideration for the Areopagus council (a kind of "senate" or "House of Lords"):

> His doctrine is based on the fundamental principle of Pythagorean psychology, that there is an essential identity between the laws which regulate relations among sounds and the laws which regulate the behavior of the human soul. Music, therefore, can influence character, especially in the young and still malleable. Among various types of melodies and rhythms, one must identify those most capable of educating the young to virtue, wisdom, and justice. In defining and analyzing the harmonia,

> Damon maintains that only the Dorian and the Frygian have a positive paideutic function because they encourage valorous behaviour in war and instill wisdom and moderation in peace (. . . Damon's) theories about the *ethos* of the harmoniae with reference to education were accepted by Plato and Aristotle, and they therefore conditioned Hellenistic and Roman thinking on the subject
>
> (Comotti 1989:31–32).

These thoughts were not realized by Damon while he was concert hall director. It is believed that Pericles, in 444–443 BCE, exiled his music consultant because Damon applied too much pressure to build a far too expensive concert hall (The Odeon), which was especially conceived for vocal performances (Comotti 1989:30–31). The hall was finished, in all of its magnificence, in 440 BCE and is considered to be one of Pericles's finest building structures, located on the Acropolis' south slope close to the Dionysus Theater.

Music was antiquity's most comprehensive, significant, and ritually communicative media form, with all the propagandist possibilities that this always contains. One might compare antiquity's music to today's social media on smart phones. Musical theory was the intellectual's tool to, in part, communicate internally and conceptually develop the medium, and in part, guide, develop, and educate – and for the politicians – manipulate the populace. Damon's musical ethos theory thusly would become a superior piece of pedagogy in democratic education. If it became this in Damon's (and Pericles and Sophocles's) own time is not known – Pericles does not mention this in his memorial speech for the fallen, when he talks about the difference between Spartan and Athenian pedagogy. But if his musical ethos theory wasn't embraced in Athens as it was in Sparta, perhaps this is the explanation for Sparta's superiority and victory in the war.

In 1938 in a series of lectures and in his book *Homo Ludens. Proeve eener bepaling van het spel-element der cultuur* (*Homo Ludens. A Study of the Play-element in Culture* 1955), the Dutch historian and culture theorist Johan Huizinga presented a thesis about play and competition as a civilizing function:

> The view we take in the following pages is that culture arises in the form of play that it is played from the very beginning. . . . Social life is imbued with supra-biological forms, in the shape of play, which enhances its value.
>
> (Huizinga 1955:46)

It is Huizinga's view that "rules" as a concept and in practice, have many of the same origins. There are no distinctions between the rules of law and the rules of play/games. Both are developed at the same time in a given culture and influence each other and the culture to such a degree that the distinction is moot. Play/games doesn't *become* culture, but becomes part of a "twin union" (Huizinga 1955:46). In the same way play/games are an integrated part of culture:

> *Poiesis,* in fact, is a play-function. It proceeds within the play-ground of the mind, in a world of its own which the mind creates for it. There things have a different physiognomy from the one they wear in "ordinary life," and are bound by ties other than those of logic and causality.
>
> (Huizinga 1955:119)

This is even stronger in music, where he finds that "the same is true, and in even higher degree, of the bond between play and music" (Huizinga 1955:120). He thus makes "the rules" or "the order" into the most essential, in that he can eliminate all forms of rank, dominance and sequence. Just as he can, with this, establish that there is no distinction between the rules of law and the rules of play/games, we can, regarding 7th- and 6th-century BCE music, say that there is no distinction between the rules of music and the rules of philosophy/government, in the sense that the rules of music theory were based on logic, mathematics and democracy. As will become apparent in this section's concluding model, the explanation of 500–400 BCE's highly developed thinking about logic, philosophy, mathematics, physics, state theory and sports, is based on the fundamental centuries old integration of the equally highly developed music and play/game theory.

Christian Dahl also has this in mind when he highlights that:

> All across Greece choir membership is considered to be an essential part of a citizen's education (*Paideia).* One can assume that this was especially applicable for the boys' choir, but not just this. Plato points out in *The Laws* that a man without choir training is a man without an education, and this perception presumably was widespread all over Hellas where, in some places, *koros (the choir)* and peideia were virtually synonymous.
>
> (Dahl 2010:65)

Musical tradition's high status was maintained through the centuries, partly because of the consistent and comprehensive music education that was pedagogically developed by music theorists and the many conservatories, and partly because it was stimulated by the comprehensive annual dithyrambic competitions at the Dionysian festivals. The choir discipline function (keeping the body fit and coordination) and the connection between intellectual and physical learning and development were of course also among the goals (Dahl 2010:65–67). But superseding all of this was the unshakable collective recognition that music was a power factor that should be respected. Dahl recreates the core of Damon's musical theories formulated by the words that Plato placed in Socrates' mouth: "There is no way to dislodge the forms of music, without it affecting the basic laws of society" (Dahl 2010:67).

Friedrich Nietzsche also conceded the great importance of the choir in *Die Geburt der Tragödie* (1872, *The Birth of Tragedy*) and in addition declares "melody's" absolute supremacy:

> *Die Melodie ist . . . das Erste und Allgemeine*
>
> (Nietzsche 1872:44)

The key to understanding the development of Athenian and classical Greece's superiority in the arts, philosophy, architecture, natural sciences and political sciences lies in music and game theory and its culture; in Athens these theories were both supported by and deeply integrated into the centuries that came before.

Theater music

The tragedians and comedic poets, who all together worked for less than 100 years, composed everything using the Damonian harmoniae model. It was possible, however, for necessary and logical innovations within this musical tradition. Only Euripides took this a few steps further. It's not surprising, since all of these poets geared their work toward a larger audience. Only comedy – which isn't to the same degree dependent on musical modernity – retained the Damonian harmoniae unchanged.

So as far as the music of the tragedies, comedies, and satyr plays were concerned, the dramatists seemed to attach themselves completely to existing tradition. Philologists' use of Aristophanes's comedies as source material, also vis-à-vis his ironic take on tragedy's musical style and genre choice, did however result in several misconceptions. We know that Aeschylus and his contemporary colleague Phrynichus, hardly excelled at "sweet songs" in the ionic tradition nor did they plagiarize Phrygian's ritual melodies, as Aristophanes otherwise unjustly claimed in *The Birds.* They chose rather to remain loyal to the Doric and Phrygian tradition's diatonic and enharmonic forms (Comotti 1989:32, Anderson 1994:119), the way music sounded in their youth, in approximately 500 BCE.

Sophocles also remained close to this tradition, though in certain areas he followed the era's musical currents:

> There is a greater variety of meter and rhythm than in Aischylus. Unusual elsewhere in dramatic lyric is Sophocles' use of such choral passages as the *hyporchema*, of monodic songs – real soloistic tunes – and of duets, and finally, the use of Phrygian and dithyrambic melodies in addition to the Dorian and Mixolydian, more commonly employed in Attic drama.
>
> (Comotti 1989:33)

There are only a few references to music in Sophocles's tragedies, and only in the context of solos or the chorus. Regarding the chorus, music is mentioned especially in connection to voice changes from hopeful to sorrowful (Anderson 1994:121).

With Euripides, it was totally different; the musical references suggests a composer completely involved in the rapidly changing music scene. (Anderson 1994:121–122). Of course he did this to target the conservative Aristophanes, who in *The Frogs* called his music whore-songs and dance music. In reality, he was creating a new form of opera, which in the 4th century BCE became very popular:

> In his work music gradually loses its traditional function as the support for the poetic text and becomes instead a means of expressing dramatic moments, the emotions and the states of mind represented in the tragedy – a new role fulfilled especially by the typical use of choral odes. Monodies, which were rare and of limited extent in the tragedies of the first period, become ever more frequent and longer, making the tragedy equivalent to a downright melodrama with arias and duets.
>
> (Comotti 1989:34)

What really got on the nerves of Aristophanes and his musical bedfellows was that Euripides now and then allowed syllables to spill over more than one node:

> This practice, common in Western music from very early times, struck fifth-century Athenian conservatives as being radical to a degree that we can scarcely comprehend.
>
> (Anderson 1994:123)

> One should keep in mind that Greek and Latin meter was based on the quantity of syllables, not on the position of stress or tonic accents, as is the case with modern Western languages.
>
> (Comotti 1989:12–13)

Though several researchers also claimed that Euripides, with his eagerness to innovate, was very much an opportunist, and in his so-called "melodramatic" tragedies – *Orestes, Helena, Iphigenia in Tauris* – he does this as a no-content librettist. Anderson cites H.D.F. Kitto for the following tirade about Euripides' melodramatic passages for the choir:

> Some of these odes are quite as empty and nearly as silly as some of Mozart's libretti; if we had Euripides' music, and Greek ears to hear it with, would it all perhaps sound as marvellous as Mozart's operas?
>
> (Anderson 1994:122)

Probably yes. Euripides did write, just like Mozart, in a political era that was filled with threatening upheavals, and for a hungry-for-entertainment public. Both Euripides and Mozart finished the old world in style – and carried themselves (that is to say their artistic production) over into the new.

The instruments

The musical instruments that were used were the four or seven string lyre (for accompaniment), the seven stringed kithara (for concerts) and the oboe-sounding wooden wind instrument (the *aulos*). Most used was the double auloi, which is fingered with one hand on each pipe and with both mouthpieces together in the mouth. This is a so-called double reeded instrument in the oboe or the shawm family and not, as the majority of philologists and theater historians call it, a flute – with a lack of scientific precision that the music historian Martin L. West calls: "The most pervasive sign of the average classist's unconcern with the realities of music" (West 1992:1).

Since the 1980s, a long list of music historians and specialists in classic music from antiquity, have earnestly attempted to warn us about this fallacy or indifference and have even achieved some results, though without what one can describe as having much impact. While *The Great Danish Encyclopedia*'s article about music in

Greek antiquity correctly describes the aulos as a shawm instrument, the rest of the encyclopedia, in several captions for images, consistently calls the instrument a flute (or spells it aul*on*). In a similar manner, an entry about alcohol talks about satyrs' plucking and pressing wine grapes "while one of them plays a double flute." In another entry about the Olympiad we see an image of a vase where three athletes are being entertained by an aulos player. The caption reads: "The costumed flute player in the middle reminds us that the Greeks used music as a means to achieve beautiful and rhythmic movements in sport." Perhaps, but on the other hand, it is certain that the vase painter consciously depicted an aulos player (see Figure 2.3).

What irritates, not to say offends, musicians and musicologists, is that the classic philologer, who adamantly defines and sustains the difference between ancient Greek and Latin, without blinking, could call an aulos or oboe a flute, even though the aulos, regarding both

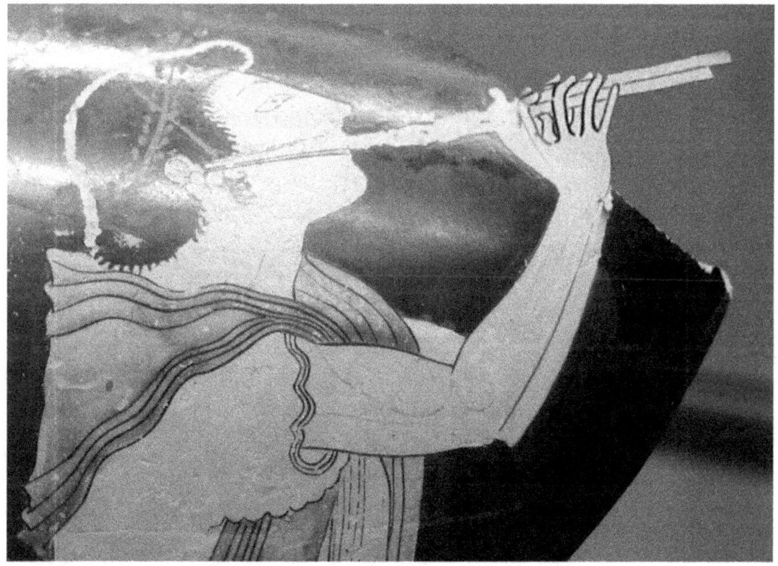

Figure 2.3 Professional aulos player during a performance with head and face strap to support the mouth pieces

Source: State Antiquity Collection, Munich, Wikimedia Commons; with my reconstruction of the double aulos

technique and sound, separates itself from a flute just as much as Greek does from Latin.

Aulos and auloi

One didn't use military instruments like the horn or trumpet for theater performances or concerts, and only rarely used percussion instruments that were intended to be used for cultish occasions.

While mastering the lyre was part of every boy's education who later as adults played lyres for entertainment at feasts and gatherings, the kithara and the aulos were instruments intended only for professional musicians. The aulos – the single as well as the double – was played by both men and women, but had a lesser social status than the lyre or kithara, which were played by the upper class. The same thing applies to the harp, which is always seen in the hands of women, and was perhaps part of a woman's education. Apart from this, the harp had no significance in Greek musical life (Comotti 1989:56–75).

Only one musician was used for the tragedies, comedies, and satyr plays – an aulos player, from whom quite a lot was demanded. However, the musicians were divided up into separate teams by lottery, so that the choreographer (the sponsor) could easily purchase the best musician (Anderson 1994:113). The aulos player seems to have been the concert master who, through his play (insertions, intonations), body rhythms, and visual instrumental selections, guided both the chorus and the actors (Anderson 1994:119).

Martin L. West describes the aulos' tone in this way:

> The instrument had quite a penetrating tone, to judge by the ability of a single pair of auloi to accompany a choir of up to fifty men. The larger sizes must have had a fairly deep voice in view of narrowness of the bore. Aristophanes represents the sound of piping by *mümümü, mümü,* and likens it to the buzzing of wasps.
>
> (West 1992:105)

West reproduces a number of characterizing adjectives that characterized the aulos' sound in that era, among them "'screezing,' or 'squawking like a goose' . . . strong, intense, forceful, sweet-breathed, pure-toned" (West 1992:105).

In addition, it is suggested that the aulos had an immediate erotic Dionysian function and appeal. Warren D. Anderson presents a choir-example from Sophocles's *Women of Trachis*:

> Almost incoherent with emotion, they cry: "I am borne aloft [sc. In the dance, by joy], nor will I reject the aulos." Now what had begun as a paean to Apollo, Artemis, and the Nymphs abruptly changes for six lines as the ecstatic women addresses the aulos directly: "O master of my soul!" For a few moments, they "*imagine* themselves to be bacchanals," as R.C. Jebb remarks. . . . "The music of the aulos," he adds, "suggests the spell of the *kissos*," the ivy sacred to Dionysos, symbol of his worship.
>
> (Anderson 1994:121)

> The aulos . . . according to Plato has the power to posses the hearer with frenzy and mark him out as being in need of religious purification. Aristotle calls the aulos "orgiastic," i.e. conducive to religious frenzy, and it is regularly mentioned (together with drums) in connection with Bacchic, Corybantic, and suchlike ecstatic cults.
>
> (West 1992:105)

The instruments are linked to a series of rituals and liminal states see pp. 98–101. Thomas J. Mathiesen cites contemporary music theorists and pedagogues about how "the auloi playing a melody for those who are mourning are the lighteners of their grief," or how weddings are instrumented by auloi and lyres among those, who are dancing (Mathiesen 1999:126–127).

Notes

There are no scores available for any of the tragedies, comedies, or satyr plays. But individual fragments with text and notes do exist (see Figure 2.4), just as there are many examples of lyrics that are put to music. It is possible, from scales, text syllables, rhythms, and theoretic musical determinations, to create music that in form and sound perhaps approaches the original. Computer generated music should contribute strongly to this. The instruments' timbre and tone can also be approached, as can breathing and fingering techniques.

[? ? I O X ⊥ U

[μή] τε ἐμοὶ μήτε ἐμοῖσ[ι τέκνων τέκνοις ἐλπὶς ἅδε ποτ' ἔλθοι

[. T [T _ Ш ?

[οἷαν] αἱ πολύχρυσοι Λυδαὶ[καὶ Φρυγῶν ἄλοχοι στήσουσι παρ' ἱστοῖς μυθεύ<ου>σαι

? ? Λ _I ? ⊥

τάδε ἐς ἀλλήλας· τίς ἄ[ρα μ' εὐπλοκάμου κόμας ἔρυμα δακρυόεν

Γ ¯[? ⊥ ? ? [T Γ T

τ[αα]ς γᾶς πατ·ρίας ὀλο[μένας ἀπολωτιεῖ;

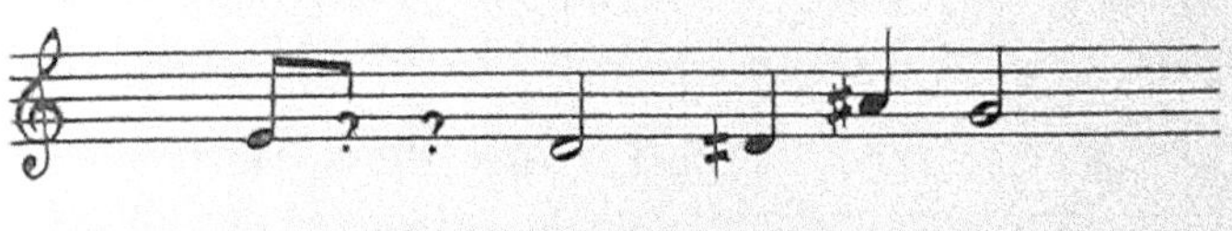

μήτε ἐμοὶ μήτε ἐμοῖσι

οἷαν αἱ πολύχρυσοι Λυδαὶ

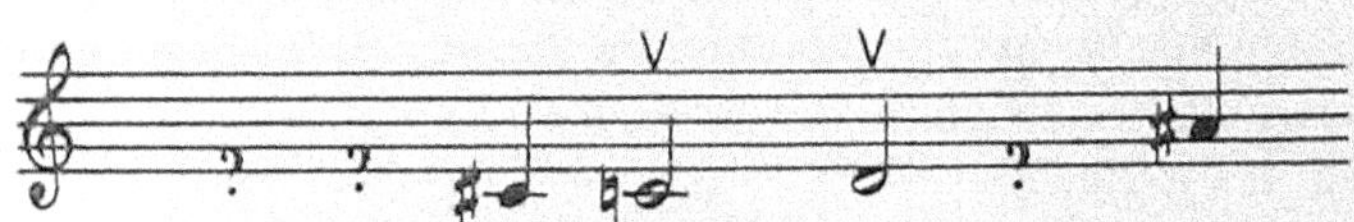

τάδε ἐς ἀλλήλας · τίς α

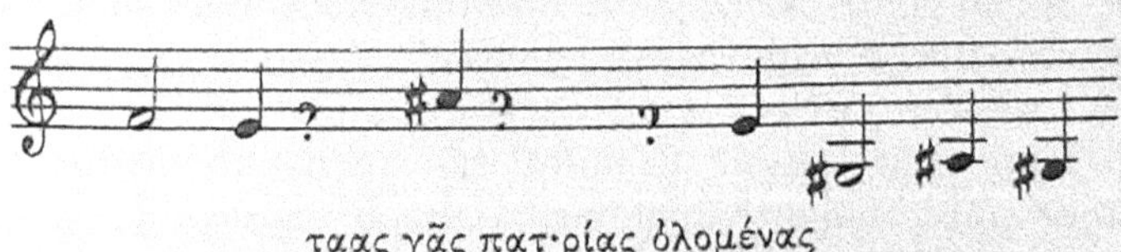

ταας γᾶς πατ·ρίας ὀλομένας

Figure 2.4 Sections of text with notes from Euripides' Iphigenia in Aulis *in the Phrygian scale (Comotti 1989:111). The Music from Euripides'* Orestes *is in both the Dorian and Phrygian scales (Comotti 1989:112).*

"The Greeks and the Romans did not know harmony, in the modern sense of the term, or polyphony; their music expressed itself through pure melodic line alone. (…) Music was simple and linear and, at least until the last decades of the fifth century B.C. functioned mainly to characterize the text in relation to its poetic 'genre,' its purpose, and the occasion of performance (Comotti 1989:12)."

Work with music from antiquity should be approached as a combination of instrumental/vocal interpretation and performance, where the dramatic text and dance is presented and developed simultaneously. The Greek theater was *Gesamtkunst* – theatrical works and performances that are presented and developed simultaneously, a form that we, despite everything, still know today. Not least, from the modern rock festival.

Dance

While antiquity's music has its theories, notes and instruments that we can relate to both concretely and in reconstruction, it's quite a different story with dance. It is true that we have hundreds of images of dancing men and women. But these are images, reliefs and sculptures that were drawn or formed by visual artists or artisans with the visual experience in mind, and for this reason alone cannot be considered as choreographically instructive or as communicatively instrumental.

In spite of this, many dance researchers and choreographers felt that they could reconstruct steps and movements by systematically selecting and analyzing the portrayed dancers. Steps and movements that can in the visual context be attributed to a specific dance with textual evidence and rhythm is, of course, much more germane than non-specific steps and movements. But the dream of putting together a longer series of contextually certain images that might be played back as film still hasn't been fulfilled.

Nevertheless, it is convincing when dance researchers juxtapose such structural and motif-like positions. In his work *Dancing at the Dawn of Agriculture* (2003), Yosef Garfinkel is able to draw a picture of the dance in the Middle East's pre-historic culture as ritual practice. He introduces this with the following point, that dance in a non-literate society, aside from the entertainment value, had a special pedagogical function:

> In periods before schools and writing, community rituals, symbolized by dance, were the basic mechanisms for conveying education and knowledge to the adult members of the community and from one generation to the next. The lengthy duration of dance depiction as a dominant artistic motif, together with its dispersion across broad geographical expanses (from west Pakistan to the Danube basin), testifies to the efficiency of the dancing motif as one of the most powerful symbols in the evolution of human societies.
>
> (Garfinkel 2003:3)

Seen in this perspective, the image is a sign, a choreographic instruction that can be read by those who can understand the language.

This leads to the question, what is dance? Garfinkel presents the following definition by the dance researcher A.E. Kaepler in his article "Dance" from 1992:

> [Dance has been defined as a] complex form of communication that combines the visual, kinesthetic, and aesthetic aspects of human movement with (usually) the aural dimension of musical sounds and sometimes poetry. Dance is created out of culturally understood symbols within social and religious contexts, and it conveys information and meaning as ritual, ceremony and entertainment. For dance to communicate, its audience must understand the cultural conventions that deal with human movement in time and space.
>
> (Garfinkel 2003:3–4, Kaepler 1992:196)

This cultic-religious starting point, which is also the most common amongst dance and antiquity researchers (Erbe 1962:12, Hjortsø 1968:60), garners criticism from Frits G. Naerebout,, who rejects using expressions like 'religious dancing," "cultic dancing," and "sacred dance.'"

> I even suggest we should do so when speaking of those occasions which could reasonably be labelled religious or cultic. Such expressions seem to imply that dances that function as part of religious life have a special character, presumably a specific movement of style. This need not be so: the context of the performance is the decisive factor. And even if a specific cultic context asks for a unique movement style, it still is not, strictly speaking, the dancing that is cultic, sacred or religious, but the occasion at which the dancers perform.
>
> (Naerebout 1997:325–326)

If dance's context is *the festival*, shouldn't it also be analyzed in conjunction with the other festival expressions – music, song, theater, poetry presentations, and sport? Naerebout sees dance simply as a ritualized performance, along with all the other performative expressions:

> [P]ublic events are in large part ritualized occasions. But it is a specific kind of ritualizing that catches the eye: dramatic theatre, dancing, music (what Schechner calls the "behaviour arts": arts

> that are actualized in performance) processions, games, sacrifice. All this dramatizing, all these displays of a theatrical or theatroid nature, all the shows that are put on, I will call performance.
>
> (Naerebout 1997:342)

Naerebout takes a sharp turn away from previous attempts at dance reconstructions with the juxtaposing of images of individuals or for that matter, complete dances, as we know them from the jars, trays, and reliefs:

> I . . . want to state boldly that no static image can assist in recreating even a single movement, let alone a sequence of movements, if that movement or sequence of movements is not known beforehand. Obviously, Greek dance movements should be considered unknown, as the reconstructionists will agree, otherwise there would not be any need to try to reconstruct such movements: a simple revival (or even preservation) would be enough. . . . The moment depicted, assuming it was done in a reasonable accurate manner in the first place, can be (and will be) interpreted as belonging to several different movements. Those who do not already *know* the movement depicted, have a mere "snapshot" and are unable to conclude with any certainty what went before and what would have followed. And even knowledge of a particular movement idiom is no guarantee.
>
> (Naerebout 1997:234–235)

Naerebout is right that the observer or reconstructionist doesn't know how the entire dance might unfold and therefore can't with any certainty insert a snapshot into its correct place. Images and sculptures of sportspeople often indicate the depicted position and placement within the process: spear or discus throwers, a few seconds before the throw, runners, at a point between start and finish, in the same way as erotic images are also more or less documentarian and process-certain. Here we are talking about commonly known rules and acts:

> Imagery, whatever its connotation, can never be considered *a priori* as consisting of straightforward depictions of once observable practice, and not even as mere *illustrations* of that other side of past reality, a society's *mental* life. Imagery is not a passive mirror produced by a craftsman/artist who is a mere conduit for extra artistic information encoded in a visual form. In real life imagery is *creative* and contributes actively to the way in which people see and structure the world around them. Images, as messages in a

> communicatory process are an integral part of the "mental universe" of every man and help structure human experience.
> (Naerebout 1997:243)

I asked the Danish dancer and choreographer Nønne Mai Svalholm to characterize and evaluate approximately 100 photographs of dancers from vases, jars, plates, and reliefs and to give her overall impression (see, e.g., Figures 2.5 and 2.6). She concluded that they depicted the

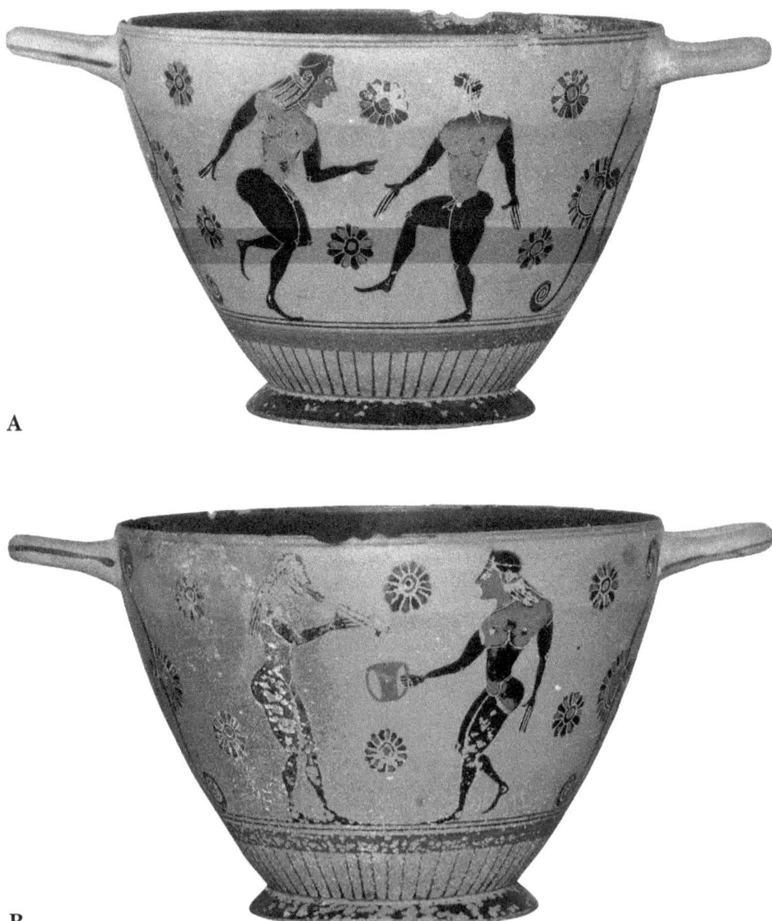

Figure 2.5 Dancing men

Source: National Archaeological Museum, Athens, photo by Spelios Pistas; © Hellenic Ministry of Culture and Sports/Archaeological Receipts Fund

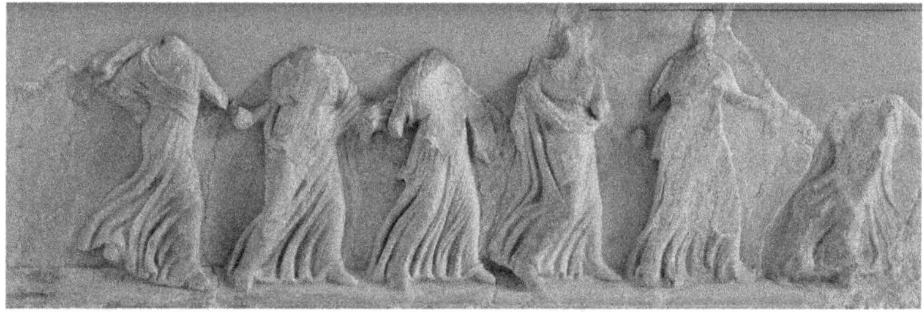

Figure 2.6 Dancing women

Source: ©Acropolis Museum 2012, photo by Socratis Mavrommatis

same body-ideal as romanticism. The visual artists/artisans depicted their epoch's ideals: What was beautiful to look at, which movements were "hot" in relation to this body and movement ideal (angles, lines, movements with positions: hands, wrists, heads, and necks).

In addition to this, Nønne Mai Svalholm concluded that the visual artists/artisans focused on gender differences and on different parts of the body: For the women, the artists focused on the shoulders, arms, hands, breasts; they are graceful, beautiful, and sensual. For the men, there was focus on their rumps and legs, on strength and power.

On the other hand, she couldn't discern any reconstructive possibilities from the rather comprehensive visual material, which confirms Naerebout's skepticism. Indirectly, Nønne Mai Svalholm told an entirely different story: The images of the dancers on the many jars, plates and reliefs, which were brought from Greece to central and northern Europe, clearly inspired contemporary choreographers and the development of "modern" ballet. Did the young Auguste Bournonville, for example, during his studies in 1820s Paris, examine the classical ideals and positions that were described by Nønne Mai Svalholm, on the salvaged classical artifacts that were the era's highest fashion? Take a look at John Keats' poem "Ode on a Grecian Urn" and his tracing of the vase with the dancing women (Figure 2.7). Here lies an exciting task for dance historians.

Theater

Buck song?

Traditional theater history (Hjortsø 1968, Erbe 1962) puts great emphasis on describing tragedy's religious genesis from Dionysian

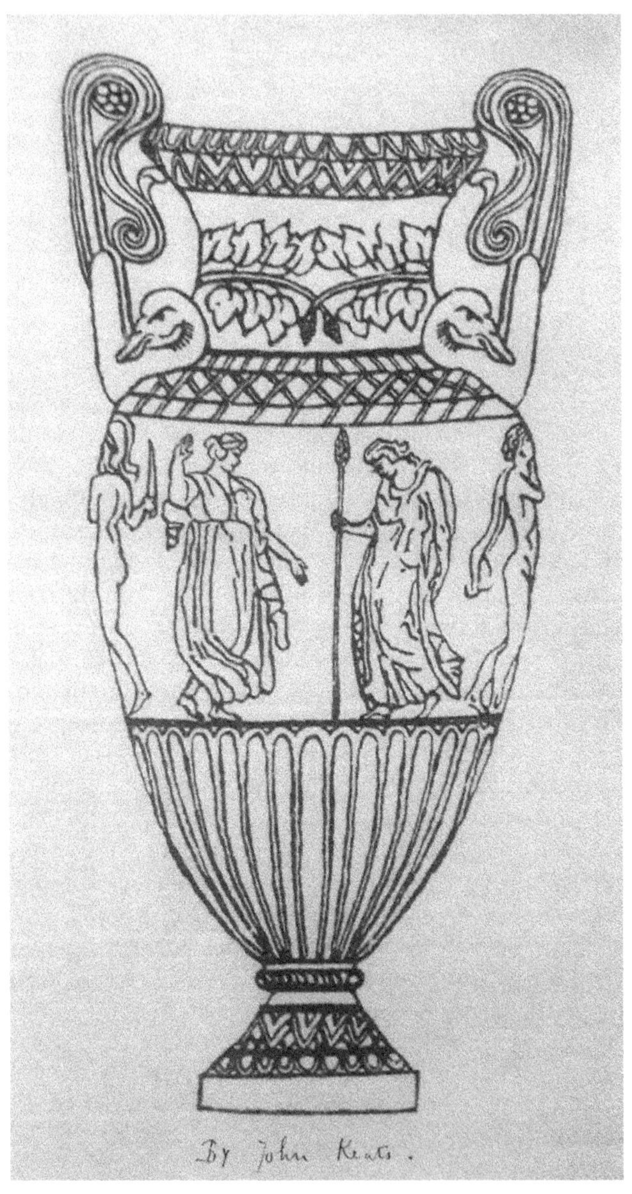

Figure 2.7 John Keats's tracing of the urn with dancing women that led to his poem "Ode on a Grecian Urn," written 1819 and published 1820

Source: Wikimedia Commons

feasts, which were held with dithyrambs or cantatas that were "performed by young men in honor of Dionysus, and consisted of dance, music, song and words. The music was played on flutes [!] and was in the Phrygian mode" (Erbe 1962:13). Then through the centuries, up to the 500s BCE, these dithyrambs supposedly developed into classic tragedy form, with actors, choir, musicians and dancers: "From what has been said, it seems plausible that the tragedy is said to have developed from the leaders of the dithyramb" (Blume 1978:22). The word tragedy is thought to be a combination of *tragos* (goat) and *odia* (hymn), that is to say, a goat or buck song. The goat was the animal that was sacrificed to Dionysus.

With these somewhat uncertain musings about the dithyramb's development, together with etymological speculations, researchers wanted to maintain the holy origins and connective tissue between the dithyramb via satyr plays to the tragedy (Erbe 1962:12, Hjortsø 1968:60). As Hjortsø formulates it: "It was in Athens that the Dionysian dance became *the tragedy* " (Hjortsø 1968:65). Researchers clearly didn't let themselves be convinced by Nietzsche's more than vigorous rejection of tragedy's alleged genesis in the dancing choir (Nietzsche 1872:48ff.).

Jørgen Mejer is also uncertain. He concludes that we don't know of any tragedy form before the dramatist Thespis in about 535 BCE:

> Of course there must have been a run up to dramatic performances before Thespis, both with the performance of choir poetry and in connection to rituals which were part of the city-state's cultic gods, but we know of nothing that might resemble the Greek tragedies. The drama must then be considered to be created by Thespis and inextricably attached to the city of Athens and its festivals for the god of wine, Dionysus.
>
> Ancient Greeks regarded neither tragedy nor comedy as pure entertainment. . . . [One performed] theater plays exclusively in connection with the Dionysian feast . . . Its unclear, however, if there is a closer connection between the dramatic performances and the actual cult of Dionysus.
>
> (Mejer 1994:152)

Jørgen Mejer's strong exhibition of uncertainty is a result of the Gordian Knot that he clenches in his attempt to separate the religious festival from the theater (The cult of Dionysius and "pure" entertainment). As we shall later see (p. 74–75), such an opposition is not to be found. Lacking this knowledge or awareness, Mejer chooses then to cut the knot with a physically visible fact:

> The more likely connection between drama, the cult of Dionysus and the city-state is also apparent in the fact that the first dramatic performances took place in Athens' Agora – a space that was at the center of the city's political life.
>
> (Mejer 1994:153)

This only proves what we already knew, that the state supported both theater performances and Dionysian festivals. It is more important to assert that the performances took place at the same time as the Dionysian festivals many other happenings and offerings of music, dance, and the potential participation in the cult's orgiastic and ecstatic displays.

Theater sport and X factor

In contrast to the lack of solid establishing evidence for the deification of the art of tragedy or the opposite there are completely concrete sources for the Dionysian feast's organization and development, especially for its overarching form of competition, the agon – with meticulous presentation of rules, participants, judging constructions, financing and production (Erbe 1962:15–16, Hjortsø 1968:71, Blume 1978:22 ff., Isager 1985:13–14, Dahl 2010:39 ff.).

The competition was led by a government official, an Archon, who was appointed beforehand for a little less than a year by the state. His duty was to choose three tragedy poets and five comedy poets and to allocate a choir for each one. Next, he had to find three sponsors, each willing to honor a dramatist and to pay for setting up their tetralogy – three tragedies and a satyr play. In addition to this, the Archon needed to find five sponsors for the comedies. Finally, he had to appoint a judging committee consisting of ten men, one from each of Attica's *fyles* (administrative districts). They are chosen for this task by lottery on the same day that the performance is to take place. We are not talking about theater-critic level evaluation here, but rather a vox pop, similar to what we know from modern TV. In order to strengthen fyle identity, each fyle was to present a trained dithyramb choir consisting of 50 men and 50 boys. Even though many of the men were probably the fathers of one or more of the boys, precisely this concurrence brought a good number of parents, grandparents, siblings and other relations to the performances. The training and facilitation (song and dance expertise, equipment, food, venues, transportation, lodging) of the dithyramb choir plus related expenses were entrusted to a local sponsor in the fyle. There was always competition to become the *choragus*, the title of the one lucky enough to be chosen, because it was in itself prestigious and when the performance became part of the festival's competition, there were also prizes for the best dithyramb choragus, comedy choragus, and tragedy choragus. Sponsorship of all the festival's dithyramb choirs, comedies and tetralogies demanded 28 rich men dressed in purple, all striving after the prize as the best choragus of them all (Blume 1978:32, Erbe 1962:15–16; Figure 2.8).

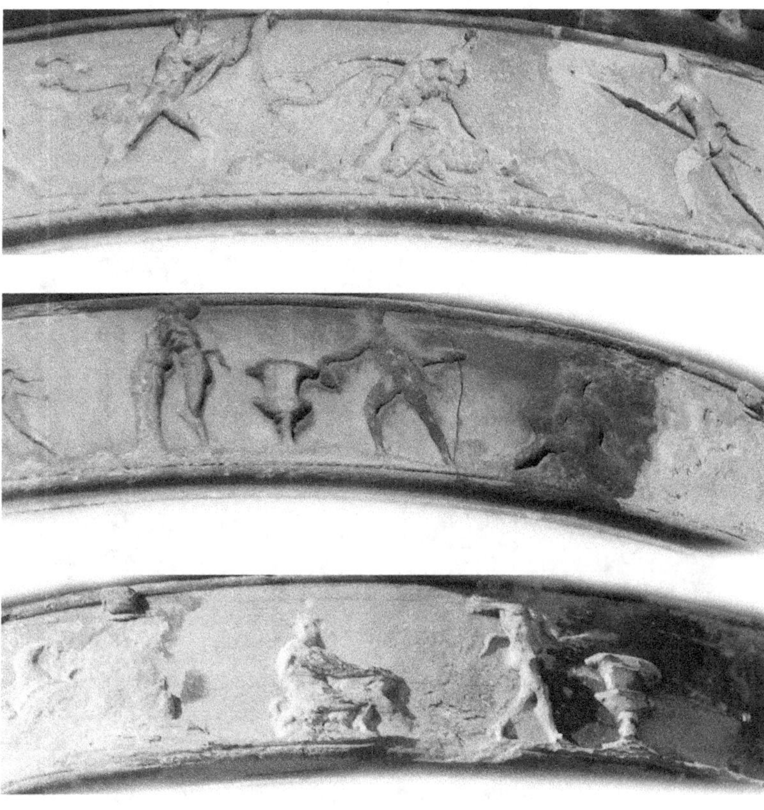

A

Figure 2.8 The remnants of a sponsor monument in Athens from circa 334 BCE erected by Lysicrates, for best tragedy sponsor with the right to monumental immortalization. As a professional showman, Lysicrates chose to decorate the entablature with a frieze that shows Dionysus in action pacifying ocean pirates by transforming them into dolphins – perhaps a selected scene from the tetralogy's final satyr play

Source: Author's photo

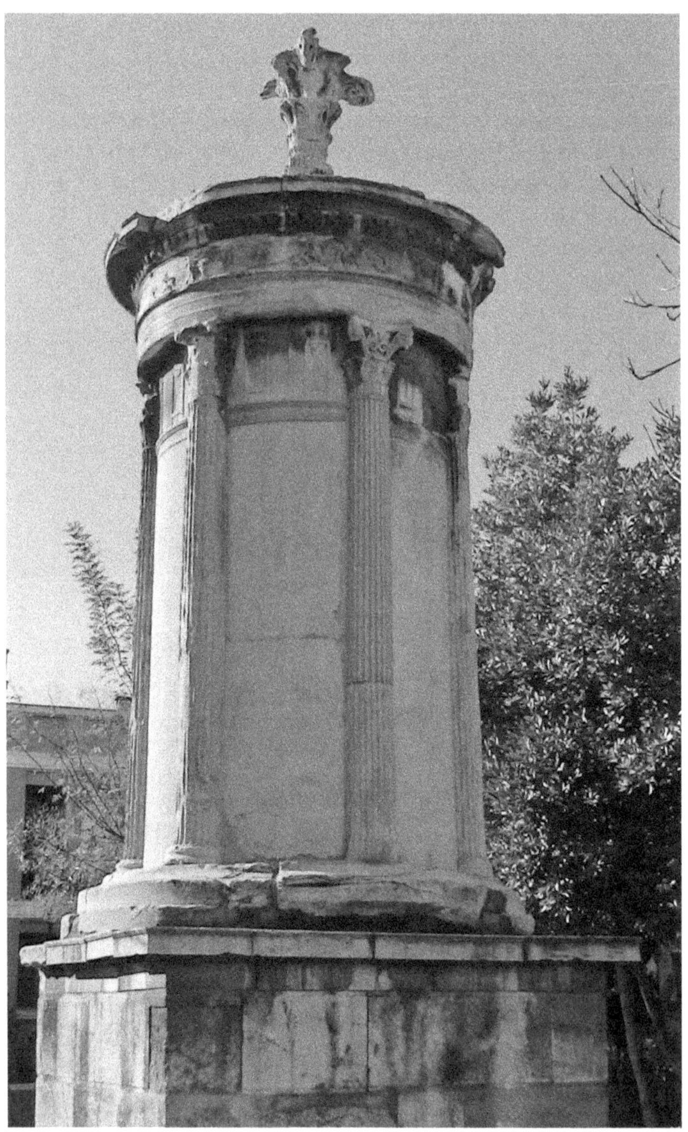

B

Figure 2.8 Continued

So, the public didn't just go to the theater for the performance's sake, but rather to watch a competition show, where they themselves had influence over the outcome. They gained this influence by applauding and throwing dried fruit, or by booing, accompanied by pebbles, to influence the judges' decisions. And the judges, who were just normal spectators from their respective fyles were, to say the least, receptive to an audience's vox pop. A divided public could easily subvert the decisions of the perhaps not especially theater-knowledgeable judges. Blume states that the Archon in 458 BCE had to resolutely ask the college of governmental strategists (who of course were among the spectators) to take over because everyone would bow to their decision – and the young Sophocles, whose tetralogy this was about, received his first prize. "The strategists unassailable authority . . . trumped the general public's artistic sensibility" (Blume 1978:41).

The strategists, like the rest of the government officials, politicians, foreign diplomats and priests, sat in the orchestra section's first rows.

How many participated in that 5th century BCE festival is hard to say. The number of seats in the 300 BCE's stone theater can't easily be translated to the older wooden theater. Though the bleacher area was somewhat smaller, there was probably place for an audience of 7,000. But what about the many people who would rather see a sports competition or hear a poetry reading or just sit with their cups in the shade? The majority of participants most certainly participated in the procession with the wooden image of Dionysus and the phallic pole. This procession ended with public dining in the stadium. If we just knew how many oxen were used for this combination of sacrifice and feasting, we could multiply this number by the approximately 110 solid portions of roast that the ancient oxen, according to contemporary knowledgeable butchers, could provide. On top of this, of course, were the goats and sheep. We could also divide the number that the sale of the oxen's hides might bring in, using the era's going price for leather. These kinds of extensive calculations have been done, but only regarding the 300s BCE, where this information is available. However, Vincent J. Rosivach, who used the same weight basis as my expert in Copenhagen's meat packing district, finds problems with this approach, because of conjectures about who was eating and how much:

> We do not know what a size of a typical portion of meat was a public sacrifice, nor whether the size of portions varied from event to event. We also do not know whether the portions were intended only for the adult male citizens, or also for their wives, children and other dependents; and if the latter, whether or not the portions varied according to the number of dependents shared in them.
>
> (Rosivach 1994:158)

The only thing we know with certainty is that when the Parthenon frieze was completed in 431 BCE, it portrayed 16 oxen and 3 goats in the segment which portrayed the procession on its way to the Panathenaic festival – a number that could feed 1,800 participants – many more than the 45 who are shown in the frieze.

So after all this, is the question only how to multiply and divide? Or is it, should we trust a comic strip at all?

The festival

The Dionysian Feast took place in the first half of the month of Elaphebolion, which runs from March to April. That is to say, the end of March. The dates were fixed to the 8th-16th Elaphebolion. In this way, one could finish up the festival with a popular assembly meeting on the day that was the month's midpoint (Blume 1978:25). Here, no consideration was given to the week or weekend!

Signe Isager, with support from Horst-Dieter Blume, has put together a festival program (Blume 1978:25–26, Isager 1985:9):

Standard program for Athens's great Dionysian feast in the classical era

8 Elaphebolion: ***Proagon.*** The participating authors present their cast of actors, choir members and musicians to the public.

9 Elaphebolion: Dionysus is brought home so the festival can begin: shortly before this, the god's cult image is carried to a shrine outside of the city, so one, on the evening of the 9th, in the glow of torchlight, can symbolically allow Dionysius to make his entry into Athens, just as he did for the first time from Eleutherae.

10 Elaphebolion: The colorful procession to the shrine of Dionysus at the foot of the Acropolis, where sacrificial animals are slaughtered. Inside the theater, the fyle competition for best dithyramb choir for men and boys. Selection of the best choragus. *Komos.* Unrestrained partying in the streets.

11 Elaphebolion: Competition for the five comedies. Selection of the best comedy writer and choragus.

12–14 Elaphebolion: Competition for the three tragedies-tetralogies, each one consisting of three tragedies and a satyr play and each one with one day at their disposal. Selection of the best tragedy writer, choragus, and actor.

16 Elaphebolion: The popular assembly meets in the Dionysus Theater, where disputes that occurred during the festival are temporarily resolved. Later, the cases can be brought to court.

Tragedy's paradigmatic function

There are various opinions regarding the deeper meaning of creating all of these dithyrambic comedies, tragedies and satyr plays. Just as there are numerous explanations regarding the theater's function, audience and interpretations. The majority of researchers support their many theories from readings of Aristophanes's comedies, drawing on dialogue and verse as more or less the barest necessary documentation. This of course, from a literary-scientific perspective, is unacceptable. Partly because we are talking about fictional characters' statements in a literary context, partly because of comedy's satirical, ironic, and humoristic dramaturgy.

In their endeavor to "make people into better citizens in their cities" the tragedy writer brings in legend and stories from Greek mythology:

> Here we see how myths are rather explicitly used as commonly applicable exemplification of humanity's existential problems, and through this, human attitudes and human reactions in critical situations . . . mythology's characters and their fates, their deeds and their mistakes (become) magnified larger than the human format and, for their later descendants, function as clear and strongly drawn examples. . . .
>
> This exemplification in a format that surpasses normal humanness one usually calls mythology's paradigmatic function. . . .
>
> In this way tragedy solves the societal, folk-educational task that this era considered as its most important.
>
> (Friis Johansen 1985:21)

Therefore, according to Friis Johansen, tragedies unlike comedies, dealt with concrete political problems:

> How much a given tragedy's message had to do with the societal form that was the Athenian listener's everyday democracy depended, not least, upon the chosen myth, which in principle could quite easily have had little to do with 400s Attic democracy. But the majority of the preserved tragedies actually had a great deal to do with the democracy's problems, even when the mythic material in and of itself didn't, to any degree, have an apparent relationship to this.
>
> (Friis Johansen 1985:21)

On the other hand, according to Friis Johansen, it is very wrong "to perceive an Attic tragedy as a kind of roman à clef where, for example, the tragic hero Oedipus "represents the contemporary politician Pericles" (Friis Johansen 1985:22). Friis Johansen could be right about this. But perhaps it is worth considering if Sophocles's Oedipus tragedy, which was written in the year, or in one of the first years, after Pericles's death, was an *auto*biographical allegory about a general and a strategist (albeit also a dramatist) who shared responsibility for his city-state's misery (the plundering of Attica and the pestilence in Athens)? Under all circumstances one clearly understands if Sophocles in 406 BCE felt the urge to appear in the role as *Oedipus in Colonus* in the hope that he might receive just a bit of forgiveness in his city of birth for the outrageous political and military mistake that he, together with the city-state's other leaders, had made and that could only lead to Athens's annihilation as a political and cultural great power – which happened, of course, two years after his death.

Phillip B. Zarilli leans into the same thing, albeit in a more positive direction, in his Case Study about Oedipus in the chapter about "Religious and Civic Festivals: Early Drama and Theatre in Context" in *Theatre Histories* (2006):

> Sophocles's tragedy centers on a plague that is afflicting the ancient city of Thebes, where the play is set. The citizens of Athens were just recovering from a plague that had ravaged their city in that year, the playwrights, performers, and producers in fifth-century Athens often presented plays that commented on current social and political problems. *Oedipus* would have fulfilled an expectation of the Athenian community. In the drama, King Oedipus must discover to have killed Laius, the former king, in order to prevent the plague from killing the Thebians. Through keen detective work and his own memory, Oedipus learns that he himself was the killer and that Laius was his father. Also in 427 B.C.E, the Athenians were fighting a war with Sparta, another Greek city-state, and they needed strong leaders who were not afraid to face the consequences of their past actions. *Oedipus* is partly a play about the need for leadership in the midst of a political crisis.
>
> (Zarilli 2006:85)

The cult of Dionysus

Gods and humans

The ancient Greeks cultivated a promiscuous system of gods; the king of these gods was Zeus, who openly practiced extramarital infidelity ad libitum with women who were both gods and humans, with all that this entailed – the jealousy, envy, and domestic spectacles. In contrast to later religions like Christianity and Islam, the Greeks didn't believe in a concept of sexual sin (forbidden extramarital relations or homosexuality), though it didn't permit polygamy. In addition, Greeks believed he/she should live life while he/she had it. There would be no life after death, as there is for both Christian and Muslim.

The world of the Greek gods was simple and instructive. The supreme god Zeus, in contrast to society's family laws, was married to his sister Hera. Together they produced Aphrodite, the goddess of love and beauty, her husband Hephaestus, the god of blacksmithing and artisans, Apollo, the god of light and song, Artemis, the goddess of nature and hunting, Ares, the god of war, Hermes, the god of thieving and trade, Dionysus, the god of wine, ecstasy and theater, and the self-generated favorite daughter, Athena, the goddess of wisdom and art.

While the other gods erected their appropriate temples at agoras, health centers, oracles, palaces and sports arenas, Dionysus was – despite being on the bottom of the hierarchy (and way out on the wings in most Parthenon pediment presentations; see e.g., Figure 2.9) – the most present of all these gods in everyday life. As a culture minister for festivals, drunken gatherings, and whoring Dionysus was there *in practice*, for men and women as well as for men and men, *in dramatics*, especially as expressed in comedies and satyr plays, and *in the visualized*, as portrayed on ceramic vases, trays, frescoes, mosaics and in sculpture. It was in Dionysus' name that one partied ecstatically, wrote pieces for the theater and dithyrambs, choreographed and performed them, danced, played and marched in processions – and on the third evening of the Feast of Dionysus, it was in his name that people participated in "unrestrained partying and dancing through the streets" as described in the festival's program (Isager 1985:9).

Der Neue Pauly, Encyklopädie der Antike (*The New Pauly, Encyclopedia of Antiquity*), however, points out that the wine-and-festival god Dionysus was neither the god of erotica nor promiscuous sexuality, stating "That exaggerated enjoyment of wine has a negative effect on male potency isn't just a modern recognition," (article: Dionysos: The Erotic), adding that images on vases rarely associate wine drinking with erotic ecstasy and dance. Nevertheless, wine was an important lubricant for the Dionysian festival and is portrayed in other vase images of, for example, wine-producing satyrs. In addition to this is what David Wiles calls the "emblem" of the Dionysian Feast:

> The story told of how Dionysos was rejected when he first visited Athens with his dangerous gift of wine, so he punished the men by condemning them to a permanent state of erection. An erect phallus thus became a central emblem of the festival.
>
> (Wiles 2000:31)

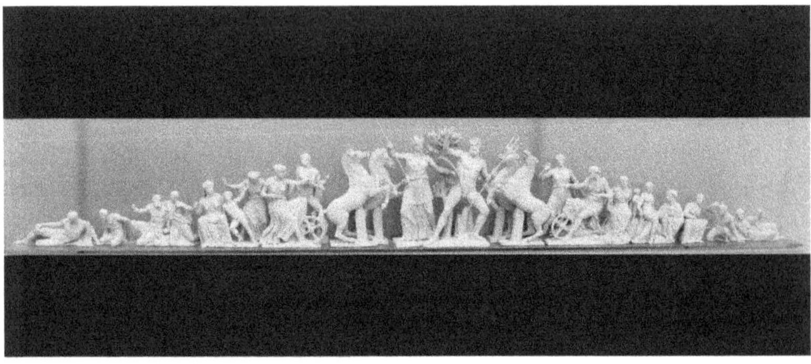

A

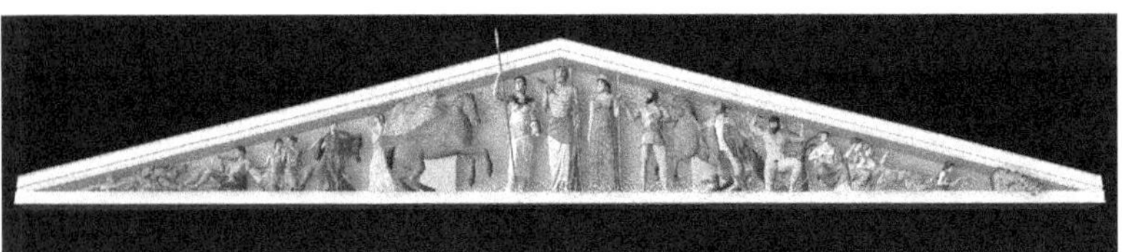

B

Figure 2.9 There has been no lack of reconstructive suggestions for the Parthenon's west and east pediments through the centuries. Above we can see a recent suggestion (based on a drawing by K. Schwerzek) from the link, Wikimedia Commons. With new insights into ancient colorations, we can now also see examples of polychromatic reconstructions of the world of the gods, here from Robert Bowie Johnson's The Parthenon Code: Mankind's History in Marble, *in the form of Homes Bryant's artistic computer generated rendering. Robert Bowie Johnson is also the author of* Noah in Ancient Greek Art *(Johnson, Jr. 2004).*

Orgy or festival?

When, at a mature age, the classic philologist, antiquity historian and gymnasium teacher Leo Hjortsø launched his little educational book *Hellas* out into the flower children's world of 1968 he didn't lack for words or images to depict the "Dionysian" for that dawning youth revolution. Using full page illustrations of vase decorations portraying embracing bacchantes and satyrs in full (if not fully erected) penis length, clutching their cups and mugs, with their feet planted solidly in the grape press, Hjortsø, with evangelist verve, introduced the 16–19-year-olds to the mysteries of the god of wine:

> The cult of Dionysus consists of faithful identification with the god – the follower himself became a satyr or another of those

> creatures that are part of Dionysus' disciples. And throughout the entirety of Greek literature and art we can track that choir of possessed, drunken, jubilant and love-intoxicated men and women, a noisy chorus, whose echoes continue to reverberate long after they have gone.
>
> (Hjortsø 1968:62–63)

The German antiquity researcher Horst-Dieter Blume, ten years later, scarcely less exuberant than his Danish colleague, also had his eye on the border-smashing and liberating power that lay in the Dionysian cult, albeit here, in a more tame bourgeois version that in the end, sluiced its way into the city-state's festival calendar:

> Dionysus seized control of minds with never before seen power. He gave people the feeling of limitless freedom, promised them liberation from the ruling forces, and those who can imagine the social conditions in the Greek Polis will certainly recognize that especially women, who were locked out of political and social life, would feel attracted to this religion. Dionysus' swarming orgiastic cult of Maenads (possessed female disciples), without hesitation, tore themselves out of their domestic prosaic closed-in existence and into the wilderness. His madness provided people with ecstasy and allowed them to fill themselves completely with the divine. A number of mythic stories show how the leaders futilely attempted to suppress this culture's licentiousness and irrationality and prevent approval of this god: the new religion's triumphant march however didn't stop. But before the 6th century BCE Dionysian cult could capture a permanent place in Athens' official festival calendar, its character had to be tamed. Actually, those solemn sacrifices that Dionysius now brought to the assembled citizenship, hardly had much to do with the nightly orgies of intoxication and violence that once played out in the free nature.
>
> (Blume 1978:14–15)

Blume could have enriched his description with Arnold Hauser's historical-political analysis of the Dionysian Festival. The two researchers are not in disagreement but supplement each other in the finest way:

> The inauguration of the cult of Dionysos by [the Tyrant] Cleistenes in Sykion was undoubtedly a move in that prince's

> political game and intended to supersede the Adrastus cult of the noble families there. The Dionysia introduced by Pisistratus at Athens was a politico-religious festival, with the political factor incomparably more important than the religious one. But the religious institutions and reforms of the Tyrants were undoubtedly based on genuine popular emotions and needs and this emotional disposition of the people was partly the cause of their success. Like the Tyrants, democracy also made a great use of religion for the purpose of attaching the masses to the new state. In the formation of this liaison between religion and policy, tragedy proved an excellent mediator, taken up a middle position between religion and art, between the irrational and the rational, the "Dionysian" and the "Apollonian" elements. The rational factor, the causal connection of the plot, is from the very first almost as fundamental to tragedy as the irrational element – religious awe.
>
> (Hauser 1989:78–79)

Blume sees the Dionysian cult as an agro-proletarian protest movement necessarily disguised as a religious movement, and as such, a breathtaking "new-belief" system for the city's oppressed women. Hauser sees it in part as a political chess move against the aristocracy and as a way to appropriate the people's trust, if not to say, a way to create a dependency on the new political system. Here, tragedy shows itself to be a most excellent medium for the fusion of religion and politics. This tragic-religious mash-up created a kind of political consensus between the people and their political leaders.

Neither does Blume believe in a pervasive Dionysus infiltration of the tragedy. God's path and the theater's path are quickly separated:

> so the statement about tragedy having nothing to do with Dionysus only took on a proverbial character. Very true that the connection to the cult remained, but the theater's worldly ingredients reveal a dialectic [*im agonalen Prinzip* (after the agonal principle)] as well as a secular component of the theater. The Greek's pleasure in competition that spurred participants to the highest level and communicated the excitement to the public, seems to speak against common conjectures about a cult drama.
>
> (Blume 1978:16)

The Dionysian here becomes a framework, albeit still festive, for theater festivals.

Theater performances are included as one of many competitions – like athletics, wrestling, races, instrument playing, singing, dancing, poetry recitals – and also dramatics, actors' presentations, production leadership and organization (the prize for best Choragus).

In this context it is important to look away from the tragedies and comedies for a moment and to focus on the satyr plays (only one satyr play survives with full text). Which is what David Wiles does. There is in fact a clear connection between these tetralogies' concluding pieces and "the Dionysian":

> Having danced in three successive tragedies, a feat of considerable athletic prowess not to mention memory, the chorpismen transformed themselves for a wild finale into servants of Dionysos called satyrs. Satyrs were part divine, part human, and part bestial, having the ears and tail of a horse and the same permanently erect phallus that Dionysos once inflicted upon the Athenians. . . . In the Satyr play a chorus of beings obsessed with drinking and copulation was inserted into the world of heroic myth, with farcical consequences. . . . The satyr play did not puncture the world of tragedy, but anchored it to the figure of Dionysos. It released the spectators from the emotional trauma of tragedy, and reinserted them in a world of celebration.
>
> (Wiles 2000:35–36)

This concept, in performance theory jargon, is called "dispersing" and was one of the many dramaturgical methods that helped unite tragedy, festivals, and democracy into a single unity.

The Panathenaic Festival

The procession

Processions were clearly a *must* in Greek entertainment culture. Whether they included phallus carriers, Dionysus figures, ecstatic women, cattle (for sacrifices and consumption) or a new outfit (for the god's wardrobe), depended entirely on the festival's objectives and rituals.

The largest festival was held in the name of Athens, the city goddess, in the warmest month (the first month on the Attic calendar), Hekatombaion (July–August). Every fourth year the budget and the arrangements were especially generous, when "The Great Panathenaic Festival" took place.

The Panathenaic Festival was (at any rate since 566/565 BCE, Neue Pauly 1996) a totally and entirely athletic betting event (like our contemporary horse races), where sportspeople could win prizes consisting of containers of olive oil, but where the betting public was at its core. As a prize the olive oil was hardly considered as a supplement to the victorious athletes' large consumption of massage oil. On the other hand, the container itself, with its painted sports motifs, was a beautiful reminder of the sportsman's victory. In addition to the athletic competitions and betting there was also betting pertaining to music, song, dance and "rhapsodic Homeric citations" (Pauly 1996). Whether there was also betting in the theatrical arena, as declared in several older presentations and encyclopedias (Salmonsen 1915), remains uncertain.

The Attic festival has naturally enough been portrayed in a variety of ways up through the 20th century, all depending on the prevailing religious, moral, political and philosophical conditions in a given era or in a given nation. In the beginning of the last century, the connection between religion and athletics has been rather vigorous, as we can see here in Salmonsen's Conversational Encyclopedia (1915–30):

> crowds moved in a Procession to the Temple while holy Songs were sung (Hymns, Paeans); Hymns were sung in Shrines by a chosen Choir that had previously rehearsed them. But it wasn't just Sacrifices and the holy Songs performed on Festival days that drew People to the Sacred Sites.
>
> From the remotest Past, Greeks felt deep Pleasure in Physical Agility and Athletics: already in Homer's Poetry, Betting Contests that were regularly held during various festival occasions were mentioned (Odysseus's Visit to Alkinoos – Patroclus' Funeral). It is only natural then, that Betting Contests early on were connected to religious Festivals, and that one attributed to the Gods the same Joy of Watching the Power of the Body and Athletics that earthly Spectators felt themselves: Betting Contests . . . as such, became a part of cultivating the Gods. The Choir's Performance of the holy Songs that were also accompanied by Dance movements, in many situations, took the form of Betting Contests, because several Choirs Performed, competing with each other; and Plays evolved from these musical Betting Contests (at Dionysian Feasts, though also other festivals). At the Shrines, which became the seat for the great Feasts, in addition to Temple and

> Alter, other special Buildings and Facilities were erected to Use for the various Betting Matches, namely Racing Tracks (Stadiums) and Theaters. Of the largest Festivals celebrated in Greece, we can name the Olympic, Isthmian, Nemean and Pythian Games as well as the Panathenaic Festival.
>
> (Salmonsen 1915, entry: Greece)

The goal of this bit of positivistic fiction prose is to allude to the athletic betting contest's natural affinity to religiosity, as well as to suggest that the theater's origins were in the musical betting contests. As we have seen previously, there is no way one can talk about such a linear development, but rather we need to look at an era's dialectical contemporary conditions, and the fact that it was ideology and politics that steered both theater art and festivals, as well as the athletic contests' development and settlement. The Salmonsen article perceives and presents "the procession" as a physical expression of "religiosity" and not as a ritual that has to be carried out before the participants in a unified collective consciousness can reach the heart of the matter: the betting contest.

The modern German antique encyclopedia, *Neue Pauly*, also notes only that the festival "which was held every fourth year as an athletic festival by the Pan Hellenistic imperium" extended over several days and found its form in 566/5 BCE, and mentions, among other things, prizes awarded in the form of oil in jars. *Neue Pauly* further states that we only know about the musical betting contests from pictures on vases and that the procession which was made up of the city's various citizenry and social groups, started at the Kerameikos entrance and continued across Athens's Agora on up to the Acropolis, ending at the Athena Polias statue (which from 432 BCE stands in gold and ivory in the newly erected Parthenon Temple. Later processions ended at the Erechtheion Temple, finished in 406 BCE). Here was the place for sacrifices and for distribution of meat. Thereafter, a nightly ritual of a dancing girls' choir took place. There was emphasis on the young girls carrying out sacred duties like *kanephoroi* (basket carrying). In addition to this, representatives from the "colonies," allies and the oppressed masses were there, underscoring the festival's imperial function. The purpose of the procession was to bring the beautifully decorated outfit to the goddess. "The Procession, which can be seen on the Parthenon Frieze, is usually purported to portray this procession," concludes *Neue Pauly*, "but the details of this reference are very debatable" (Pauly 1996, entry: Panathenaia).

Here the *Neue Pauly's* editors and the author who wrote the article don't say more than what they completely believe in. Nevertheless, or perhaps because of this, they feel compelled to inform us that the Parthenon Temple's frieze is not a documentary film. For *Neue Pauly* the portrayed procession is still just the physical expression of the religious event.

3 Analysis

Performance studies

"Performance," as an area of study, was established at New York University in 1980 when the Drama Department changed its name to the Department of Performance Studies, a subsection of the Institute of Performing Arts, and one of three departments at the Tisch School of the Arts at NYU. The school was named after its main sponsor, the philanthropic New York family Tisch.

Performance theater instructor and theorist Richard Schechner was appointed professor and leader of the department, which then ceased as a traditional theater-history department. The changeover had been in the works for two decades, scientifically as well as in practice, and Schechner justified it as follows:

> We believe that if the study of performance does not expand and deepen – going far beyond both the training of performance workers and the Western tradition, far beyond the analysis of dramatic literature – the academic, performing-arts enterprise constructed over the past half century or so will collapse. A happier alternative is to widen our vision of performance, studying it not only as art but as a means of understanding historical, social, and cultural processes.
> (Kirshenblatt-Gimblet 1999:2)

Since then, subjects and departments called Performance Studies or under similar names have become commonplace at more and more universities, architecture, design, and drama schools in North and South America, Australia, New Zealand, Europe, South Africa and Southeast Asia. Barbara Kirshenblatt-Gimblett, professor of Performance Studies at NYU declares that the subject

> starts from the premise that its objects of study are not to be divided up and parceled out, medium by medium, to various

> other disciplines – music, dance, dramatic literature, art history. The prevailing division of the arts by medium is arbitrary, as is the creation of fields and departments devoted to each. Most of the world's artistic expression has always synthesized or otherwise integrated movement, sound, speech, narrative, and objects.
>
> (Kirshenblatt-Gimblett 1999:1)

Performance Studies scientifically supports almost a hundred years of ethnological and anthropological research. Among the most important are the French ethnologist and folklorist Arnold van Gennep (1873–1957), whose *Les Rites des Passage* 1909 has since, in many translations, been a groundbreaking work in ritual research. Equally important is the Dutch cultural historian Johan Huizinga (1872–1945) with his epoch-making work on human play, *Homo Ludens* 1938 (see also p. 38), which he thus defines:

> a free activity standing quite consciously outside "ordinary" life as being "not sensuous", but at the same time absorbing the player intensely and utterly. It is an activity connected with no material interest, and no profit can be gained by it. It proceeds within its own proper boundaries of time and space according to fixed rules and in an orderly manner. It promotes the formation of social groupings that tend to surround themselves with secrecy and to stress their differences from the common world by disguise or other means.
>
> (Huizinga 1955:13, Schechner 1977/88:88)

With his demonstration of the meaning of the so-called "liminal phase" in transitional rituals and his theories of rituals as "social drama" the British-American social anthropologist Victor Turner (1920–1983) achieved direct influence on performance theory.

"Social drama"

In his ritual theory, Victor Turner distinguished between three types of performance: cultural performance, social performance, and social drama. The cultural performance included staged performances (theater, dance, music, etc.) which take place within a cultural convention, delimited timeframes and with clear beginnings and endings. The social performance takes place in the individuals' daily interactions and as consequences thereof. It can manifest itself by taking on roles, self-determination, norms, and behavior, especially if they contrast with the prevailing conventions. Often it expresses itself as imitations of seen or experienced cultural performances. (Turner 1982: 32–33) Turner relies on the sociologist Erving Goffman's classic *The Presentation of Self in Everyday Life* 1959. If the role becomes unclear or untrustworthy and the individual thereby comes into conflict with the cultural or self-understanding of the environment or society, confusion and anxiety arise on the micro level (family, colleagues), and on the macro level (politics, economy) crises can develop or possibly war.

This brings Turner to a definition of the social drama's ritual, which he inserts into a four-phase structure: "breach, crisis, redressive action, reintegration/schism" (Turner 1974:38). The reason why a social drama arises is due to breaches of a dominant harmony or synchronization, or division among the groups, parties, or states involved:

> In large-scale modern societies [and for that matter also antiquity's super powers], social dramas may escalate from the local level to national revolutions, or from the very beginning may take the form of war between nations. In all cases, from the familial and village level to international conflict, social dramas reveal "subcutaneous" levels of the social structure, for every "social system," from tribe to nation, to field of international relations, is composed of many "groups," "social categories," statuses and roles, arranged in hierarchies and divided into segments.
>
> (Turner 1982:10–11)

Antiquity's social drama

From Turner's definition and conceptual expressions, it is not difficult to denote the 5th century BCE ancient Greek society as a "social drama": After Greek Asia Minor and the Ionians, with help from the rest of Greece, rebelled against the Persian occupation force in 499 BCE, Persia attacked the Greek city-state union several times. But in 480 BCE the Persians were finally turned back. Then, the two leading Greek city-states, Athens and Sparta, each established their own defense federation, which was redefined in 431 BCE as attack organizations for a war ending in 404 BCE after a Persian-Spartan alliance. After this, Athens ceased to be a significant economic, political and cultural city-state power.

During this period, Athens's leading politicians could all be described as cultural personalities and supporters of peace and freedom. But their handling of the escalating crisis that the Greek city-states were in for decades before the war, during the war and up to its conclusion, was marked by the fact that their political and military actions were in stark contrast to their otherwise peaceful outlooks. In the following quote, Turner attempts to formulate the complexity of their problem:

> Social life, then, even its apparently quietest moments, is characteristically "pregnant" with social dramas. It is as though each of us has a "peace" face and a "war" face, that we are programmed for cooperation but prepared for conflict.
>
> (Turner 1982:11)

When we insert the Athenian politicians and cultural personalities into Victor Turner's ritual theory, we see how a coherence is created from their seemingly disparate actions and expressions.

When Pericles – Athens's most influential statesman, by virtue of his annual re-election as "strategist" from 444 BCE to his death in 429 BCE – in the winter of 431/430 BCE, held a memorial speech for the city-state's first fallen soldiers in the civil war, his behavior with this speech was a "cultural performance." He delivers this speech as a staged monologue, played for an invited audience (politicians, representatives of allies, city notables, and parents of the fallen) within a delineated timeframe and with a beginning, a middle, and an end. Using the grieving parents as a serious frame of reference, he can justify the deceased's deaths by establishing criteria of success such as: Athens's democratic constitution, the city's festivals and competitions throughout the year, durability, military strength (including Athenian training as a positive alternative to the Spartan), art and science, as well as Athens as a Greek pioneer. In conclusion, he recommends that the young parents should breed new children; the old parents are encouraged to enjoy the honor of the efforts their sons have made to the state (Hjortsø 1968:108–111).

In this way, Pericles inserts the fallen soldiers into a ritual where the war is an indispensable necessity for maintaining the state's material and spiritual power and success. Leaning into Victor Turner's scheme of social drama, his speech performs the "redressive action," which is an ongoing necessity during a crisis. To ensure impact and credibility, he executes his cultural performance as a social performance in the role of statesman, a role both he and the public are familiar with and trust. The fictitious message (that death is honorable and necessary for maintaining the state's successful criteria for lifestyle, entertainment, art and science, governance and economy) is embodied in a well-defined social and political role. This allows him, for a while, to set aside his war mask and act with his peace mask. In this way he manages to bring his audience into the ritual's "liminal phase" (in the middle, between two thresholds, the last of which requires courage, fidelity, conviction, character strength and overcoming), where he can intercept possible criticisms of the actions that led to the crisis, that is to say, the war and the loss of the fallen. And through this confidence building speech, he can lead his audience over the threshold and beyond into the post-liminal phase.

Pericles, however, is himself both an active and integrated part of the social drama. He was a pivotal decision-maker in the Athenian war strategy and thus, also responsible for it. As long as his function, roles, and performative expressions are connected, he awakens confidence. On the other hand, if cracks occur, his credibility disappears, as happened in the following year, when the Popular Assembly declared itself dissatisfied with or directly disagreed with Pericles's defensive military strategy (commitment to the fleet rather than the infantry) and fined him.

If we look at the four dramatists that we know today in relation to social drama, they all deliver cultural performances as either tragedies, satyr plays, or comedies. In addition, Aeschylus presents a social performance as a military officer and Aristophanes in his capacity as a district representative. Euripides expresses himself exclusively in cultural performance. On the other hand, Sophocles, like Pericles, is involved in all three forms of performance, as a major supplier of tetralogies (cultural performances), with his public roles: general, finance council, strategist, epidemic commissioner, director and actor (social performance) and as a decision-maker and general in Athens's wars (social drama).

Seen in the perspective of social drama, a performance-theoretical analysis of Sophocles's surviving tragedies will bring forth completely new interpretations and contexts. Sophocles was *both* a co-producer of his state's social drama, with all the losses, horrors and threats of doom this entailed, and a major producer of its tragedies for representative and entertainment use.

"[T]he roots of theatre are in social drama" writes Turner (1982:11). Applying the following quote to Sophocles's overall dramatic and socio-political activity draws a sharp and empathetic self-portrait of the great entrepreneur and dramaturge of the war:

> By means of such genres as theatres, including puppetry and shadow theatre, dance drama, and professional story-telling, performances are presented which probe a community's weaknesses, call its leaders

> to account, desacralize its most cherished values and beliefs, portray its characteristic conflicts and suggest remedies for them, and generally take stock of its current situation in the known "world."
>
> (Turner 1982:11)

Ritual and entertainment

The importance of *play* for ritualized entertainment is evident. The Greek festivals, whether more emphasis was put on music/dramatics or sports, were carried through and fundamentally understood as play, with the connotation of play used as a marker for the game's competitive forms:

> Ritualized behavior extends across the entire range of human action, but performance is a particular heated arena of ritual, and theater, script, and drama are the heated and compact areas of performance. However, something else is involved in performance, and that is *play*. Play also occurs in many species, but nowhere is it so extensive, nowhere does it permeate so many activities, as in human beings.
>
> (Schechner 1988/2003:99)

The greatest obstacle for previous antiquity research was the unwavering belief that "ritual" came before "entertainment," that music, dance, performance (tragedy, comedy, satyr plays), readings and sport more or less all grew out of ritual. It's not just wrong; it interferes with our understanding of the nature and cultural function of performance:

> The entertainment aspects of gatherings are of special importance. Western thinkers have too often split ritual from entertainment privileging ritual over entertainment. It has been accepted wisdom to assert that ritual comes first (historically, conceptually), with entertainment arising later as a derivation or even deterioration of ritual. Ritual is "serious," while entertainment is "frivolous." These are prejudiced culture-bound . . . entertainment and ritual are braided together, neither one being the "original" of the other. At celebratory gatherings people are free to engage in behavior that would otherwise be forbidden. Even more, special non-ordinary, ordinary, otherwise forbidden, (frequently promiscuous) behaviour is not only permitted, but encouraged, prepared for, and rehearsed. Behaviour during carnival combines

> or alternates with prescribed spontaneity with large-scale public performances.
>
> (Schechner 1977/88:172–173)

Performance grew out of an event that developed from a ritual with rules and patterns. Within this development, a number of contests and games emerged, games displaying both aesthetic and physical behavior. If you followed the Dionysian procession through Athens's Kerameikos gate, you would inevitably end up eating roast beef in the stadium, enjoy the sight of young girls dancing, listen to and vote for (if you were a man or boy) or even participate in the choir competition. You would allow yourself to be led through the streets and the night's drunken orgies, while the aulos droned on around you and excited the dancers. During the daylight hours, it would be all about winning the X-factor in theater poetry, performance, aulos-playing, reading and sports – all part and parcel of the genre of "interactive performance."

Whether this was ritual (let alone religion) or entertainment, hardly anyone wondered.

"Restored behavior"

According to Richard Schechner, the process described by this concept is the most important of all types of performances:

> Restored behavior is living behavior treated as a film director treats a strip of film. These strips of behavior can be rearranged or reconstructed; they are independent of the causal systems (personal, social, political, technological, etc.) that brought them into existence.
>
> (Schechner 2002:28)

All we perform or see performed are repetitions of previously experienced or learned actions, now perhaps in new combinations, contexts, or reproductions. The performance theorist and theater historian Marvin Carlson clarifies this as follows:

> The recognition that our lives are structured according to repeated and socially sanctioned modes of behavior raises the possibility that all human activity could potentially be considered as "performance", or at least all activity carried out with a consciousness of itself.
>
> (Carlson 1996:4)

This eternally recreated performance and experience behavior is completely central to the maintenance of recurring parties and festivals. The audience must see and experience the known and the tried, the orthodox and the classic, in modern repetitions. Thus, the audience is brought to a place where performance and experience melt together into the question of: performance as experience or experience as performance?

Referring to Victor Turner, two of the subject's theorists, D. Soyini Madison and Judith Hamera, write:

> Once an experience presses forward from the field of day-to-day it becomes the incentive for expression; it is then no longer a personal reality but a shared one. What we experience may blossom into expression whether in the form of story, gossip or humor on the one end, or poetry, novels, theatre, or film on the other. "The experience now made into expression is presented in the world; it occupies time, space, and public reality. Experience made into expression brings forth reader, observer, listener, village, community, and audience."
>
> (Madison and Hamera 2006:xvi–xvii)

The leaders of the Dionysus Festival select, organize, and produce theater experiences from performance-theoretical concepts. All considerations – conscious and unconscious – refer to this great theory complex. Not as a recipe or list or a summary, but as a social, cultural, and philosophical knowledge and recognition resource that can answer all the good questions – if one knows how to ask them.

The performative space

The explanation for the many misconceptions or contradictory accounts of antiquity's festivals, tragedies and democracies from the 5th and 4th centuries BCE Athens, lies in the canon classicists have built over the last 200 years: the story of a people who by 19th and 20th centuries measures, reached sublime heights in business, commerce, architecture, art, theater, philosophy, science and politics.

The problem is simply that the canon was incorrectly screwed together from the start. And despite overwhelming discoveries and analyzes ever since, it's only with great difficulty, if at all, that we have been able to shake off its fundamental fallacies

I will therefore conclude the first part of this book by providing a coherent explanation and by establishing a communication model that shows in a number of "performative spaces" how canonized research categories and encyclopedic "topics" have constituted themselves both *in* theory and practice and *as* theory and practice through the centuries back to the 5th and 4th century BCE Athens.

But let's begin by repeating Richard Schechner's doctrine that ritual and entertainment are one: "entertainment and ritual are braided together, neither one being the 'original' of the other" (Schechner 1977/88:172–173). This means that at all times, whether it be a tribe, a population, a people, or a nation, a universe or collective consciousness exists of a *whole* that contains a wide range of aspects or genres of ritual and entertainment. In Greece (like most other places in the world), we know of such wholes in small and large measures. But precisely in Greece, these aspects and genres are both rich and highly interacting within the whole, in the form of a natural religion or with natural religious elements, myths, music and song, dance, narrative, pictures and sports. This ritual unity was implemented in the 7th century BCE, as an active part of the development of city-state structures throughout the Greek region, in a number of more firmly ritualized practices – most notably ritual feasts with music and dance, and celebrations with sports competitions. At the same time there was a combination of ritualized theory and practice, namely the music conservatories and the music schools, which during the 700 and 600s BCE were created in all major cities, but also in several smaller towns. From these schools and conservatories, all music theory and musical commerce was disseminated by an established communication system (which the sports competition advertisers also used) across the country. But it was also in these schools that theoretical mathematics and physics were developed through the practical-theoretical employment of sound and timbre, rhythm, intervals, scales, strength, and intonation – and in physics, especially through experiments with the instruments' strings, holes, boxes, and tubes.

The disciplinary order and logic that is at the heart of music theory frees up the possibility of abstract practice-related thinking in other areas of existence. The combination of the ritual's constantly practiced transformation of thoughts, consciousness, condition, marital and social functions also enables development and changes of rules and logic, as we consistently see in music and sport, where the game and the rules change over time, but are constantly moving toward the increasingly simple, clear and understandable – always with the purpose of achieving happiness, victory, fame and oblivion.

The code of Dionysus

It is in this ritual configuration that democracy as thought and practiced social form becomes an alternative to oligarchy. On its way to becoming a structure for the great powers with colonial and allied federation status, the ritual of the Athenians, in earnest, arrives at its highest potency with integrated ritual and entertainment. This is implemented into, but never separated from, a whole system of social and political rules of behavior – rules that prevented the eradication of entire family lineages as well as individuals, but that also would consistently be able to place responsibility and take action to safeguard the privacy that ensured the Athenian man his freedom and rights.

Thus, "Athenian democracy' " came to be the ritual that was both born from and intertwined in entertainment genres (to which also the scientific belonged): festivals, dramas, song, dance, philosophy, and the natural sciences, pictorial art, sculpture, architecture, and sports.

The festivals – the Dionysus Festival and the Panathenaic Festival – evolved through the 5th century BCE to be precisely the performative space that could contain all rituals and all entertainment (all genres), implemented with rules, play and games that covered all social and political activities. The festivals, which were music and dance-borne, were legitimately supported by the music theory that had both created the festival's theater forms (the tragic, the comic, and the satyric music theater) and the thought structures for scientific knowledge, such as mathematics, physics, logic, philosophy, acoustics, and architecture.

The fact that democracy was not seen as an independent capacity in "the performative space" is because its political decision-making and executive rules and powers were abolished in 322 BCE by the Macedonian occupation power. On the other hand, the festivals and the other entertaining and scientific genres continued, as did the private and internal democratic rules of behavior.

J.R. Green indirectly supports this when pointing out the need to observe the many facets of theater and the fact that "it changed, perhaps quite radically, during the course of the fifth century." And then he continues on the wavelength of Arnold Hauser, noting that

> the Dionysia and the theatrical performance that went with it were closely linked to the democracy of Athens, and they surely served to foster the democracy just as the democracy in its turn served to foster the festival and its theatre.
>
> (Green 1994:12)

The code of Dionysus

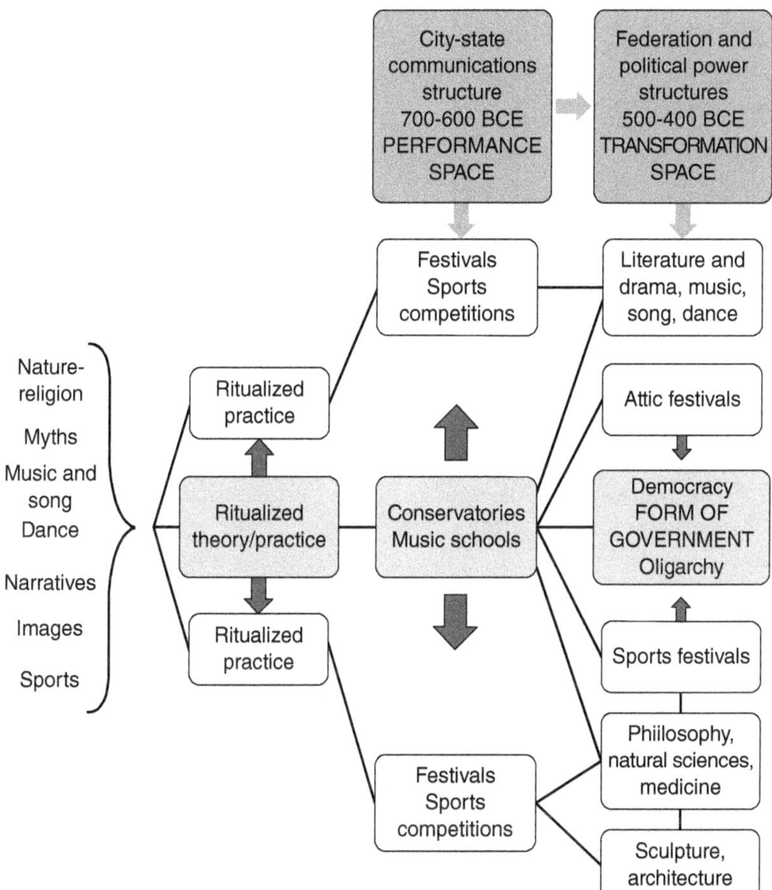

Figure 3.1 Communication model for the city-state's performance space

Richard Schechner, in his essay "Toward a Poetics of Performance," sets out three objectives that clearly also apply to the Dionysian performance, as it was integrated into Athenian democracy, and then outlines them:

- To maintain friendly relations.
- To exchange goods, mates, trophies, techniques.
- To show and exchange dances, songs, stories.

Further more, I think these performances followed rhythms familiar to us in:

- Gathering.
- Playing out an action or actions.
- Dispersing.

(Schechner 1988:175–176)

It is in the "Dispersing" phase that recognition and hence social regeneration takes place. David Wiles quotes Richard Schechner's statement: "The basic polarity is between efficiency and entertainment, not between ritual and theater" and continues:

> Schechner reformulates the old ritual/theatre divide because his ideal is a theatre capable of changing people. Greek plays portray *efficacious ritual practice*, which become in a sense rituals within a ritual. Greek plays may also be described as *efficacious myths*, shaping the way the Athenian audience understood rituals which is performed outside the Dionysia.
>
> (Wiles 2000:37)

One is tempted to name this "powerful myth" about the particularly Athenian "societal gene" – created precisely by religion and myths, music and song, dance and narratives, images and sports – and then ritualized in theory and practice in a performative space to only later be transformed and constituted into permanent institutions.

One could call it the "Code of Dionysus."

4 The Roskilde Festival

The livestock fairgrounds

Through the last 1,000 years, the Danish provincial town of Roskilde near Copenhagen has been known as the old Viking capital, and the city's splendid cathedral (from 1175 CE) has maintained its position as the church for royal funerals, uninterrupted since the 15th century.

In 1969, the city would add a Viking ship museum as an international attraction, but in 1995, it became indisputably clear that the Roskilde rock music festival, celebrating its 25th anniversary, had overtaken the position, not just as Roskilde's largest international cultural attraction, but all of Denmark's as well. Today this festival lasts for more than ten days.

As a modern festival phenomenon, Roskilde comes in the wake of the American Woodstock Festival in 1969 and its follow up in 1994, as well as similar European rock festivals. Many new festivals have come into being since the Roskilde Festival started in 1971, in Denmark as well as in Europe, but many of these had to quickly fold. Today, the well-functioning festivals are run commercially according to business and experience-economic principles. The Roskilde Festival does this too, of course. But on the other hand, as an organizational form, it seems to be composed of equal parts Athenian ancient festival and Danish club culture.

In the summer of 1971, three young people, two of whom were local high school students, arranged and put on a successful "Sound Festival," as they called it. Despite this festival being well attended, the relationship between expenses and revenues was so markedly negative that new paths needed to be found if they wanted to continue. One path was created by embedding the festival's economy in a foundation – the Roskilde Foundation of 1965, whose purpose was (and is) "to support initiatives that benefit children and young people, and to support humanitarian and other generally charitable, non-profit, cultural work" (Encyclopedia 1994, the Roskilde Festival's 2018 annual report). From the festival's re-launch in 1972 and up until its 25th anniversary, attendance numbers grew from between 10,000 and 30,000 to 100,000. In the last decade, this number has fluctuated between 70,000 and 90,000, until the numbers in most recent years have risen again to 100,000, which includes 80,000 full festival attendees and 20,000 with one day tickets. In addition, up to 40,000 volunteers, media professionals, musicians, technicians, and suppliers are attached to the festival.

Of course, the Roskilde Festival's organizational structure has developed over the years. In the years following a name change in 2004, the Roskilde Festival was managed by the "Roskilde Festival Association." This organization consisted of members who had participated as volunteers for the "Roskilde Festival Association." Membership could be achieved by 24 hours of voluntary work, plus a fee of 50 Danish crowns per person per year. The Board of Directors, Chairman, and Deputy Chairman were elected or confirmed at the annual General Assembly. The director was responsible for the festival, assisted by a management group, consisting of him or her, together with the festival's development manager and music director. The director was appointed by the board. In order to respect the applicable regulatory requirements, the "Roskilde Festival Association" established a commercially managed fund, "The Roskilde Festival Foundation" that in turn ran four subsidiaries, which together with the "Association" and "The Foundation" constituted the "Roskilde Group." The subsidiaries could support the Roskilde Festival financially.

Today the whole organization is assembled under the mantle of the Roskilde Festival Group, which is the unified designation for both the Association and the Foundation, and for the Foundation's daughter company, the Roskilde Culture Service A/S.:

> The Roskilde Festival Group consists of three boards of directors: one for the Roskilde Festival Association, one for the Roskilde Festival Foundation and one for Roskilde Culture Service A/S. All board members are volunteers. The collaboration between the boards is coordinated by three chairpersons chosen from each respective segment of the Roskilde Festival Group. The boards of directors also employ an executive who is responsible for the day-to-day management of the Roskilde Festival Group.
>
> (Roskilde Festival's annual report 2018)

Currently, day-to-day management and the directorship consists of a CEO, a CFO and a spokeswoman. Employees are divided into six departments that handle the work, the planning and development of "organization and culture," "the program," "commerce," "communications," "participants" and "urban planning and production."

The Roskilde Festival is also supported financially by several sponsors. These sponsors express interest then are selected by the festival management according to various criteria, including ethical. The Roskilde Festival has a close and mutually binding practical collaboration with the Roskilde Municipality. The municipality's politicians and officials are invited to the festival. The same applies to ministers, parliamentary politicians and ministerial officials, as well as regional politicians.

If you were to visit the Roskilde Town Hall during the festival period for ordinary expedition or for a meeting, you would notice that not only employees, from the office staff to department heads to the municipal director, but also several city council members and the mayor will all be wearing the current year's wristband affording them entry to the festival area; yes, a fair number of folks get the special bracelet that offers access to the Media City at the heart of the festival center.

Research situation and methodology

As mentioned in my introduction (p. 8), when it comes to the Roskilde Festival the research situation is quite different from what we have seen for the Dionysian Festival. While the ancient Greek festival, up until recent decades, has been exclusively explored and described by classical archeologists, philologists, historians (with classical antiquity as focus), philosophers, and art and architect historians – and later, theater scientists, music technologists and dance scientists, the Roskilde Festival has been described and analyzed by sociologists, anthropologists, cultural geographers, economic scientists (including "experience economy" scientists), literary scholars, culture and art scientists, modern ("rhythmic") musicologists and performance scientists. In addition, there are journalistic representations.

One could say that while the classical sciences have taken a patent on the Dionysian Festival, the modern social sciences and performance sciences have patented the Roskilde Festival. Naturally, this is due to the fact that study of the former depends on written sources and archaeological material, while the latter can be studied in full function every year, with live artists, organizers, and participants in performance. There are also no gaps or lack of material documenting the Roskilde Festival's 50-year existence. Eyewitness reports by participants in various media formats from all the festival years are legion. In addition to this, we can retrieve information and statements from the changing CEOs, programmers, and spokespeople Leif Skov, Henrik Rasmussen, Rikke Øxner, Esben Danielsen, and Signe Lopdrup, which we completely or to some degree don't have from Cleisthenes, Pericles, and Lycurgus. Plus, we have access to significant statements by contemporary performing artists such as Burnin' Red Ivanhoe, Dr. Hook, Pearl Jam, and Bob Dylan, which we also lack from Aeschylus, Sophocles, Euripides and Aristophanes.

The basic works of reference for the ancient festival, such as, for example, *Der Neue Pauly,* is matched by the modern rock festivals' own websites and Internet sources like *Wikipedia.* In addition, archive material and artifacts are being constantly added to the growing number of rock museums around the world. For example, the Museum of Pop Culture (MoPOP) in Seattle, the Rock and Roll Hall of Fame and Museum in Cleveland, Memphis' Rock N 'Soul Museum, The Beatles Museum in Liverpool, Rockheim in Trondheim, the Pop Center in Oslo, the British Music Experience in London – and Denmark's Rock Museum, which in 2016 opened in Roskilde near the festival site with the Norse name Ragnarock. Ongoing research into Danish rock history is available in the form of several encyclopedias and presentations: Torben Bille's *Danish Rock Encyclopedia 1956–2002*, 2002, Per Reinholdt Nielsen's *Rebel & Remix – Rock's History* 2003, and *Rock in Denmark: Studies in Popular Music from the 1950s to the Turn of the Millennium* 2013. The most famous Danish books about the Roskilde Festival are not translated into English: Anders Rou Jensen's *Between Dreams and Screams. Roskilde Festival 25 Years* 1995, Erik Jensen's *At Roskilde* 2003 (both authors are rock reporters for the Danish newspaper *Politiken*), as well as Gitte Marling and Hans Kiib's *Instant City @ RoskildeFestival* 2009.

In the ancient Mediterranean world, one knew as much about the Greek Dionysus and sports festivals as the modern world today knows about the Roskilde Festival. That knowledge was simply not preserved to nearly the same degree – here, and only here, lies the difference. Today we collect, record, communicate and store all knowledge, in principle forever, and use it if we can manage to get an overview of the vast amount of information and sources. Many of the tools of the modern sciences mentioned earlier, however, have already done a great deal of work in the form of in-depth analyses of the Roskilde

Festival's economy, organization, physical-logistical structure, music program, and concerts. We can therefore go directly to the analysis of the festival, as an interactive aesthetic performance rooted in time, place, and common action, within the social and political framework that we usually define as a constitutional parliamentary democracy.

Methodologically, it's all there: Roskilde Festival came into existence at the same time as the development of a number of newer methods of analysis – especially in literature and linguistics, but also the new cultural theories originating from or as a critique of the interwar philosophical schools (for example, the Frankfurt School). A number of socially oriented philosophers (see introduction p. 3) have produced unifying and dialectically incorporated alternatives to former positivist and Marxist methods, which since the 1980s have emerged as modern aesthetic, philosophical, and sociological theories; and since 1990 also as performance theory.

My task then will be to describe Roskilde Festival's history – its contextual creation, institutionalization, structure, dynamics, and forms of expression, both as cultural and social performance. In addition, I will analyze a number of political, economic, legal, administrative, organizational, artistic, and performative categories, and develop a "Code of Roskilde" which can be compared to the "Code of Dionysus" using the communications model I previously presented.

My desire is to demonstrate a wide range of organizational, structural, and aesthetic similarities (with 2500 years distance) between the two festivals. In each of the festivals' historical performative spaces these similarities constitute, and ritually and politically explain, the festivals and their contexts. The parts of my analysis that show possibilities for refinements and innovation, for facilitation of administrative, organizational and political practices, as well as aesthetic-performative potentials, can be transferred from the ancient festival to the modern festival. This is my contribution to the Roskilde Festival's continued existence and active business.

Music in time – time in music

The Roskilde Festival, like its contemporaries in Europe and the world, has its own story, which does not go back to Dionysian feasts, medieval and Renaissance carnivals, Wagner's Bayreuth festival or George Wein's Newport Jazz Festival (which began in 1954). Nor can we use Anne-Marie Autissier's explanation, where in just four and a half lines, she inserts 1970s rock festivals into a general development with "tourist appeal, the establishment of minority cultures, the promotion of contemporary work, and openness onto different styles of music" (Autissier 2009:31).

The late 60s and 70s rock festivals are the result of the sociological-demographic reality and the aesthetic paradigm shift embedded in that particular economic-political construction we call the "1960s' welfare growth and the cold war" (see Harsløf 2000:465ff, 1989:3ff). In Denmark, as in most other European countries and the United States, the birth rate increased in the years 1943–48, and in Denmark it almost doubled from approximately 50,000 to more than 90,000 young people per year. A greater percentage of these new citizens started a professional education or a high school education than in previous generations. In the 1960s these "baby boomer" children accounted for about 450,000 young people, approximately one tenth of the total population. Even if not quite as extreme, similar proportions could be found in most other European countries and the United States. This resulted in increased pressure on universities, seminars, art and architecture academies, technical schools, conservatories, and film and theater schools.

While young people's "soundtrack" in the 1950s was predominantly popular music ("pop") and revival jazz and, to a lesser extent, classical music, newly composed music and modern jazz, the all-dominating youth-musical genre in the early 1960s became *beat* music. Beat came out of England in 1960 from a Liverpool group called The Beatles and then later, The Rolling Stones, who came out of London in 1962. But more and more groups soon appeared – The Kinks in 1963, The Who in 1964, The Doors in 1965 – and with major concert tours across Europe and the United States they represented the epitome of youth culture music. Not only were the sound, voice and performance ideals different from that of pop and jazz, the texts were shaped as poetry with both content-related "messages" and linguistic and literary markers. In addition, these groups performed on the stages in metropolises and in big city forums and venues as well as concert halls where the management dared to let them perform. The encounter between the artists and their audience, "the fans," often exhibited itself as a state of ecstasy during the concert itself, and almost always exploded afterwards into disturbances, as they were known from soccer matches. In addition was the unmistakable imprint that the singers and the musicians left on the hotels where they were staying. Alcohol and euphoric substances were an integral part of both the lifestyle and the performances. The photos on the album covers also revealed the godlike status that their audience attached to them. The cover of The Beatles' *Sgt. Pepper's Lonely Hearts Club Band* (1967; see Figure 4.1), famous

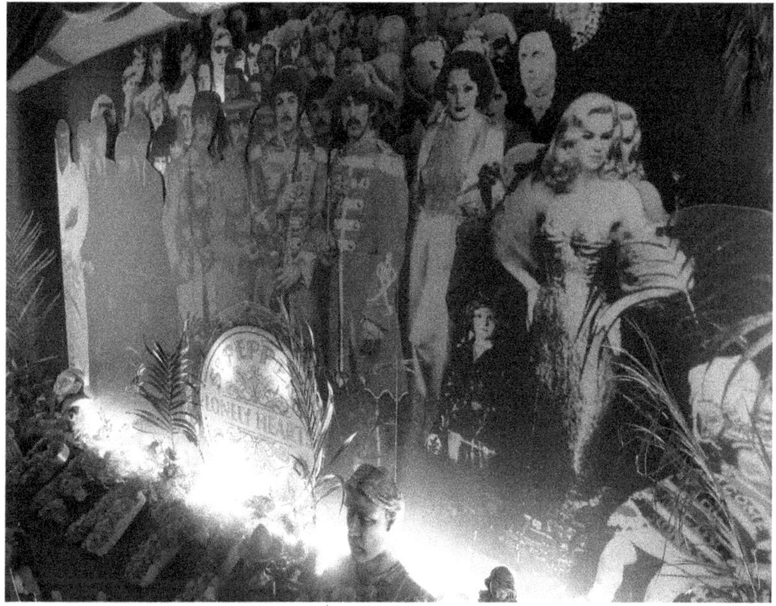

Figure 4.1 The motif for the album cover of Sgt. Pepper's Lonely Hearts Club Band recorded in 1967, The Beatles Museum, Liverpool

Source: Wikimedia Commons

ever since, where the four artists pose in pastel-colored 17th-century full length jackets á la The Three Musketeers and D'Artagnan, surrounded by previous and contemporary celebrities, including Marilyn Monroe, Laurel and Hardy and themselves as school boys in brown jackets and ties. The scene is their own mausoleum.

In 1964, beat music ran up against American rock 'n' roll and created American rock music which, with strong inspiration from Bob Dylan's "folk music" laid the groundwork for the hippies' "folk rock." So-called "acid rock" or "psychedelic rock," in text and sound, expressed the consciousness-expanding effect of narcotics as did the band names that played this music, such as the Jefferson Airplane and the Grateful Dead. This implacable, insistent musical and youth-cultural development was primarily due to fractures in American society, which emerged more and more clearly throughout the 60s. Not least of these fractures was the broader public's inability to deal with the almost incomprehensible "cold war" with its nuclear threats and the division of the world into NATO and the Warsaw Pact, followed by the American military engagement in Vietnam, accompanied by domestic civil rights demonstrations and marches that culminated in the assassination of Martin Luther King in 1968. However, what was difficult to understand for the general public was quite evident to most intellectuals and artists.

American popular music took its social and political reality and turned it into aesthetic content in sound, text, and live performances, and it now took root in the millions of young people on campus. The guitarist Jimi Hendrix traveled to London in 1966 and formed the Jimi Hendrix Experience there. And it was in England that political-psychedelic rock evolved toward the avant-garde experimental with "garage bands" like the Velvet Underground.

In Denmark, in the late '60s, we developed internationally known groups such as the Young Flowers, Burnin' Red Ivanhoe and the Steppenwolves in 1967, then Alrune Rod and Savage Rose in 1968. In terms of form, content, and expression, these bands referred to the English and American groups mentioned earlier. In the so-called "youth rebellion" that followed, rock was the music of rebellion, and just as the "rebels" tried to abolish all authority and dissolve all hierarchies, the rock band demonstrated a collective, non-soloist musical expression. Here there were no leaders nor other appointed agencies – the band names seldom referred to a single musician or the number of performers.

The '68 youth revolution

Like other great historical events, the youth revolution acquired its year and month – "May 1968," and what followed is today part of every high school history curriculum.

Worldwide, one might say that the rebellion began at the University of California, Berkeley with the Free Speech Movement in 1964, followed by San Francisco's "Summer of Love" in 1967, then spread like sparks igniting ancient gunpowder depots throughout Europe; most effectively and most covered by the media was Paris and Berlin.

Scientifically speaking, the sociology of the student rebellion has the greatest historical interest. Especially in Paris, for a month, a never before (or since) "student-worker relationship" emerged and an apparent cooperation agreement between the student organizations and parts of the trade union movement was established. Herein lay the politically explosive, which led President De Gaulle to mobilize both the military and the police. Because of the fear that with this kind of organizational understanding between the working class and the young intellectuals, the power structures of capitalist society could fracture to such a degree that a new political paradigm could arise and change the western world. It was precisely this fear that united the political parties and the trade union leaders in a head-on rejection of such a partnership. In spite of various political and economic post-war rationales, however, the party leaders, employers, executive officers, and trade union bosses had to jointly fight this anti-authoritarian insurgency.

A great deal of research has been done looking into "middle class sociology" and the "student recruitment" of the 1960s, in order to find an explanation for the uprising. The massive baby boomer generation, improved finances and prospects of full employment for college graduates all received the honor or were blamed for what the German educational sociologist Oskar Negt has condemned as "the historical localization of student and youth protest movements" (Negt 1988). Negt and many others deny the importance of *ideas* and obviously don't have the fantasy to imagine the transformation of anti-authoritarianism into politics at the same time in different parts of the world – which also included Eastern Europe and Japan, in addition to the United States and Western Europe.

It is precisely this "simultaneous" aspect that is interesting about the 68-revolt – that an idea can be qualitatively politicized in the same way and at the same time in university cities around the world. Usually this concept is used to understand and analyze uprisings such as the French Revolution in 1789 or the Reformation of the 1520s. In 1968, the uprising was about the demolition of the 100-year-old positivist knowledge and research tradition, which neither the two world wars nor a Russian revolution had influenced. Therefore, critical thinking was at the center of the revolt at the universities, while social structures were at the core of the movement as a whole (Harsløf 2000:466).

But the rebellion itself was a performance, even with its very own music. One might say, with reference to Friedrich Engels in 1841 (1968:482, 485), that what Beethoven's music meant, as a unifying national idea, for Germany, rock music, as creator of a collective identity, meant for the youth culture uprising. During the late 60s and early 70s, Europe and the United States witnessed the emergence and growth of mainstream and experimental films that also stirred the pot. American films like *The Graduate* (1967), *Easy Rider* (1969) *One Flew Over the Cuckoo's Nest* (1975), Antonioni's *Zabriskie Point* (1970), together with Jean-Luc Goddard and François Truffaut's French New Wave, offered a collective visual consciousness and sound track for the 68ers. In addition, throughout these years, Europe and the United States witnessed the emergence and growth of an imaginative and experimental group theater that as 'The New Theatre Movement' more or less set the scene for the youth revolution.

The movements

The 68 revolution indeed, became another movement. But it was composed and characterized by a variety of political interests and social preferences. The strongest of these was the anti-Vietnam war movement, but also resistance to NATO, the European Economic Community, nuclear weapons, and nuclear power plants were persistent objects of protest.

One of the highly visible organizational results of the anti-Vietnam war movement was the emergence of the publishing house and bookstore, Demos (Demos is the Greek word for 'folk'). Demos published all the theoretical background material, books, and pamphlets necessary for proficiency and/or discussion use, as well as a number of recordings. Several other alternative publishers also sprouted up, publishing books, magazines, records and posters, which had never before been published by older publishing houses or sold in existing bookstores.

The anti-war movement was front page news because of the frequency of its demonstrations. There were numerous occasions to gather and meet: The Socialist Culture Front held major festivals, Scandinavian group theaters met at the Nordic Group Theater Festival, there were women's festivals and, in Denmark, island summer camps.

The last grew out of what was initially, in Denmark, called "the red-stockings movement." From this came new attitudes and forms of association, new roles, and role distributions. The "women's movement" acquired an ideology, a practice, and then also a theory. At the universities, the theoretical aspect of articles on women's history, literature, theater, and music was strengthened.

The Isle of Wight

The world's first rock festival seems to be the one that was held on the Isle of Wight southwest of Portsmouth in the English Channel in August 1968. One of the organizers, Ron Smith, remembers the initiative as follows:

> The IOW pop festivals came about as a result of the Isle of Wight Swimming Pool Association, of which I was a member, wanting to raise funds. It was suggested we employ a fundraiser. I said I knew someone; that person was Ronnie Foulk. We then proposed, after some discussion with [his brother] Ray, that we have a pop

> festival. The committee allocated £750 and we set about putting a festival together.
>
> (*Wikipedia* 2011 and www.helium.com "The History of the Isle of Wight Festival" 14 September 2011)

This festival, like the two that followed, was organized by the three Faulk brothers (Ron, Ray, and Bill) at three different locations on the Isle of Wight. The musical top name was the singer and guitarist Marc Bolan and the festival attracted 10,000 participants. The festival's website (2011) describes Bolan's performance as follows:

> Sitting cross-legged on a flat bed truck, Marc warbles Tolkien-like fairy tales of elves, magicians and romany soup as half of Tyrannosaurus Rex. The setting is a cold stubble field, near Godshill (where the ley lines meet) to a hippie throng gathered for a now legendary one day event. The first great UK rock festival.
>
> (Isle of Wight Festival's homepage 2011)

In 1969, where participant attendance was estimated to be 150.000–250.000, the headliner was Bob Dylan:

> The most famous recluse in the world is tempted out of retirement to head up a three day event at Woodside Bay, and amazes everyone with his short hair, baggy white suit and country ways. He blinks shyly at the massive crowd, acts bashful and polite, and sings his heart out, backed by the brilliance of the Band.
>
> (Isle of Wight Festival's homepage 2011)

Among the other performers aside from Dylan and The Band was The Who.

In 1970 – with Jimi Hendrix the star among other rock, jazz, beat, soul international stars like The Who, Miles Davis, The Doors, Ten Years After, Emerson, Lake & Palmer, Joni Mitchell, The Moody Blues, Melanie, Donovan, Free, Chicago, Richie Havens, John Sebastian, Leonard Cohen, Jethro Tull, Taste, and Tiny Tim. This festival was attended by more than 600,000 people. This crowd, which, at the time, was considered the greatest assembly of people ever, had legal regulatory consequences that for a number of years put an end to the island's festivals:

> The unexpectedly high attendance levels led, in 1971, to Parliament passing the "Isle of Wight Act" preventing gatherings of more than 5,000 people on the island without a special license.
>
> (Wikipedia 2011)

The festival's homepage described Hendrix's performance as follows:

> The highlight of the biggest ever live music event seen in the UK, at East Afton Farm, Jimi comes on round midnight to give everything he has left to give. It is his last major performance – within three weeks he is dead. Opening with a distorted version of "God Save The Queen," he looks troubled, but sings and plays with a savage grace. Someone sets the stage on fire after his set, like a wake for the 1960s.
>
> (Isle of Wight Festival's homepage 2011)

The almost 250,000 people who showed up for the 1969 festival didn't seem to bother the House of Commons, nor did anyone worry that the little channel island might in 1970 sink under the weight of the 600,000 spectators. Neither of these provoked the Isle of Wight Act. It was rather Jimi Hendrix's deconstruction of the royal anthem that united the majority.

Woodstock

In 1969, the year after the first Isle of Wight Festival, four young men from totally different backgrounds joined forces in Manhattan to try to initiate a rock festival on Long Island. The location changed because of various obstacles during the planning phase and instead was moved to the Woodstock area, about 90 miles north of New York City.

The only reason that this festival is connected to the Isle of Wight festival by American rock critics is because of the curiosity that Bob Dylan's house happened to be close to the planned festival area. Dylan left his house (and Woodstock) the day before the festival's start to travel to the Isle of Wight to perform there.

American rock writers rightly or wrongly do not attach any importance to the European festival for the Woodstock Festival. Dave Laing even thinks that the Woodstock Festival inspired the Isle of Wight Festival: "The Isle of Wight Festival was widely regarded as sharing the 'love and peace' vibe of Woodstock itself" (Laing 2004:6). Laing apparently cannot imagine that the same "vibe" could oscillate in both Europe and the United States at the same time.

The author of the home page Woodstock 101, Dave White, suffers from the same American provincialism; under the heading "Four Days that Changed the World" he writes:

> The history of Woodstock is the history of the turbulent '60s in microcosm. It was all there in a muddy pasture on an upstate New

> York dairy farm: the Vietnam war, the distrust of government, the culture of sex, drugs, and rock music. Our Woodstock 101 encompasses the event, the music, and the people of the 1969 Woodstock festival.
>
> (White: homepage Woodstock 101)

What Dave White obviously means when he says "the world" is the US-world. In this way, he does not grasp what I would call "the global festival effect 1968–1970": The Rock Festival era begins with the Isle of Wight (10,000 participants), continues with the Isle of Wight and Woodstock in 1969 (150,000–250,000 and 400,000–500,000 participants) and finishes its first phase in 1970 with the Isle of Wight (600,000 participants).

It is this festival paradigm that changes the world. One is tempted to call it a dialectic: Bob Dylan, who might have appeared in the US, went to Europe and made the festival there famous. So famous, that Hendrix, one year after having played "The Star-Spangled Banner" for 40,000 acid rock spectators at the Woodstock Festival, repeated the success with "God Save the Queen" at the Isle of Wight Festival for 600,000 participants.

When Dave White and others believe it was Woodstock that changed the world, it was because of the media attention for the festival from a documentary directed by Michael Wadleigh and edited by, among others Martin Scorsese. The film was screened at the Cannes Film Festival in May 1970 (two months before the August Isle of Wight Festival) and, although it did not receive any awards there, it provided the Woodstock Festival with an almost iconic afterlife in the United States (where the film received an Oscar), Europe, and several other parts of the world.

It was this film in combination with the successful Isle of Wight Festival in 1970 (and not 1968 as Marie Autissier writes) that allowed many "rock music events" to jump on "the bandwagon" (Autissier 2009:32–33). The explanation, however, is that the media attention to Woodstock made Jimi Hendrix a superstar at both festivals – at the same time:

1968
Isle of Wight (10,000)
Marc Bolan

1969	
Isle of Wight (150,000–250,000)	Woodstock (400,000–500,000)
Bob Dylan	Jimi Hendrix

1970	
Isle of Wight (600,000)	Woodstock: The Movie
Jimi Hendrix	

In addition to this is the fact that two famous bands performed at both festivals: The Who played at the Isle of Wight in 1969 and 1970, as well as at Woodstock in 1970. The Band played at the Isle of Wight in 1969 and Woodstock in 1970.

It wasn't a pool association like the Isle of Wight or any other existing local organization that initiated the Woodstock Festival. The four initiators – John Roberts, Joel Rosenman, Artie Kornfeld and Michael Lang – are described by Dave White as "a military man, a lounge band guitarist, a record label executive, a rock band manager."

> Lang and Kornfeld became pals at their first meeting, in which Lang was looking for a record deal for a band he managed. The two began brainstorming plans for a recording studio in the pastoral setting of upstate New York in a little town called Woodstock. To introduce it, they envisioned a small festival that would include a rock concert and an art fair.
>
> (White: homepage Woodstock 101)

Already in 1969, Woodstock was known for its rock musicians and as a hippie town, and the lack of a professional recording studio could be remedied by the establishment of a regular festival. This became decisive for the four initiators. The plans were for a concert to run over three days, not an actual festival. The expected crowd was set high, between 50,000 and 100,000, high in relation to the 40,000 Miami Pop Festival's crowd in 1968. This elevated figure created logistical problems for the Woodstock area. However, the organizers managed to rent 600 acres on a cattle farm near the small town of Bethel, and to overcome the concerns of the committed artists about the questionable concert conditions, they offered double fees. Among these bands and artists were Joan Baez, Ravi Shankar, The Band, Blood, Sweat & Tears, Janis Joplin, Carlos Santana, Butterfield Blues Band, Jefferson Airplane, Canned Heat, Joe Cocker, Country Joe and The Fish, Creedence Clearwater Revival, Crosby, Stills, Nash & Young, The Grateful Dead, Arlo Guthrie, The Who, and Jimi Hendrix.

Under the heading "What Went Wrong . . . and Right" Dave White writes:

> The business plan was based on sales of tickets and concessions to 50,000 or so people. When ten times that many people showed

> up, the meager security contingent couldn't keep them from climbing fences or simply walking in without paying.
>
> It didn't take long for food supplies to run out, and for sanitary facilities to become completely overwhelmed. And nobody had counted on rain falling throughout much of the festival, rendering the pasture a muddy mess and delaying or shortening performances.
>
> Largely undaunted, attendees happily shared their food, drugs, booze and sexual partners with those who were without, and frolicked in the mud. The organizers eventually made back the $2.4-million they spent on the festival, but only when they started getting money from record sales and a successful film documenting the event.
>
> (White: homepage Woodstock 101)

Here we have the code words for success: the explosion of the estimated number of participants, extraordinary access, lack of food, inadequate sanitation, rain, and mud, community sharing of food, drugs, booze and sexual partners, good record and cinema sales. Of course, there was also the all-star parade of performers. Every American who participated in the Woodstock Festival not only denotes it as the experience of a lifetime, but also as a landmark international historical event. Facts relating to the Isle of Wight festival the following year with information on The Band's, The Who's, and especially Hendrix's performance for a much larger audience is completely displaced by the myth of Woodstock. Such a myth wasn't generated by the Isle of Wight initiators and therefore the Woodstock myth triumphed. Today, the Woodstock festivals are in every encyclopedia. The Isle of Wight festivals receive much less space.

Later, Carlos Santana, who appeared at the Woodstock Festival, proclaimed this myth's historical and human significance:

> At Woodstock I saw a collective adventure representing something that still holds true today. When the Berlin Wall came down, Woodstock was there. When Mandela was liberated, Woodstock was there. When we celebrated the year 2000, Woodstock was there. Woodstock is still every day.
>
> (Lang 2009: dustcover's backpage)

The three Woodstocks

Thus Carlos Santana, with almost lyrical humanism, expresses the paradigmatic function of the rock festival as a kind of "Woodstock's spirit." The festival lives in human consciousness as a collective adventure, which is transformed decade after decade toward new historical "freedoms."

The music journalist and author Dave Laing expresses similar thoughts in his article "The Three Woodstocks and the Live Music Scene" (Laing 2004), but here in the form of an analysis of the real circumstances that created the myth: "The three Woodstock events in the context of the evolution of live music and its business over the period linking 1969 to 1999 and beyond" (Laing 2004:1). In particular, the following three aspects:

> The evolution of music festivals and their status as carnivalized spaces; the development of the live music business, especially the move from entrepreneurship to corporatization; and finally the "deterritorialization" of the live event through sound recordings, films and television.
>
> (Laing 2004:1)

The Woodstock Festival in 1994 was advertised as a 25th anniversary, and although it attracted less than 300,000 participants compared to the 400,000–500,000 in 1969, the organizational and logistical scenario was the same: organizational and economic chaos, 100,000 free admittances, lack of parking, rain and mud, abundant supplies of brought in beer and drugs.

On the other hand, an entirely new scenario was born: corporate sponsorship (Pepsi) as well as sponsorship from co-producing record companies (PolyGram, Diversified Entertainment):

> The amplification set-up included 500 loudspeakers, 200 microphones and 12 miles of audio cable. The event consumed 9 megawatts of electricity. Production costs were over $30 million, including fees of over $300.000 for leading performers.
>
> (Laing 2004:2)

With this super professional equipment, the festival could be broadcast directly to the entire United States and, in the form of video recordings, to 26 TV networks that sent it out to 98 countries, plus satellite TV that broadcast it to 30 African nations. The TV rights alone brought PolyGram $12.5 million. Woodstock II was thus preprogrammed as a myth in production for pecuniary purposes.

Leading up to the festival, the record companies sent out earlier releases with the performing artists on the market – including four albums with Jimi Hendrix. And Warner Bros. released a new version of the movie *Woodstock: The Movie* – as a "director's cut."

In July 1999 the 30th anniversary attracted 190,000 paying participants and 25,000 who got in for free, all together half as many as Woodstock in 1969. All performers were new in relation to the two previous festivals, except for a large screen projection of Jimi Hendrix's performance in 1969 – including Limp Bizkit and Red Hot Chili Peppers. Nor was there the strong sense of collectivism. "Love & Peace" and compassionate respect were no longer represented.

The festival was covered by MTV (pay TV) and afterwards Sony released a double album *Woodstock 99* (Laing 2004:4).

Laing's point as well as the entirety of his production dramaturgy shows a 30-year development from collectivism and "Love & Peace" to individualistic self-realization, violence, and rape. For the highly monetized and media-covered Woodstock II, collectivism and the peace ideology survived, albeit with the participants as extras in a global media show. But Woodstock III revealed the festival or genre-specific violence that isn't connected to the commercialization, the media coverage, organizational or weather-related problems. It relates solely to the musical genres that are performed. These genres included hardcore punk, heavy metal, metalcore, grindcore, grunge, and rock. "Moshing," "slamming" or "slam dancing" take place as close to the stage as possible (the pit), where the dancers hit, kick and slam into each other (or into the audience outside the circle), often accompanied by "crowd-surfing."

Gerhard Falk and Ursula A. Falk give this description of the phenomenon in their book *Youth Culture and the Generation Gap*:

> The purpose of slam dancing is to promote aggression. This includes the use of traditional "four letter words" while bouncing off the people, without necessarily hurting anyone. Some slam dancers are more aggressive than others. These faster dancers are called thrashers. There are videos by bands called "Minor Thread," "Suicidal Tendencies" and "Red Hot Chili Peppers" which include this activity. Teenagers report that they get a thrill from slam dancing and enjoy the closeness with other people.
>
> (Falk 2005:192–193)

However, already during Woodstock III in 1999, the groping had evolved into rape. Several festivals and bands in the years that followed took a stand against the "mosh pit" and introduced something that, for the festival universe, was unthinkable – a ban. The band Pearl Jam allowed a poster to be printed with the following text:

MOSHING AND CROWD
SURFING IS **PROHIBITED**
DURING TONIGHT'S PEARL
JAM PERFORMANCE
PARTICIPATION IN THESE
ACTIVITIES WILL RESULT IN
EJECTION FROM THE
VENUE WITHOUT
POSSIBILITY OF RE-ENTRY

THANK YOU FOR YOUR COOPERATION

In a historical section "Woodstock and the Outdoor Music Festival" Dave Laing rightfully criticizes the English music sociologist Simon Frith's critique of the 1969 festival's staging, which Frith believes, had "dramatized the total separation between rock's performers and consumers" (Frith 1981:222, Laing 2004:6). Laing emphasizes the importance of the "carnivalesque" and "Dionysian" dimension of the outdoor festivals:

> The dimension is closely linked to the fact that, for most audience members, the key thing is to be present at the event as such, not necessarily to see or experience a particular act. The latter is the motivation to attend a concert, not a festival. The carnivalesque dimension is evident in numerous testimonies from participants in events stretching from the rock festivals of the 1960s to the raves of the 1990s.
>
> (Laing 2004:7)

With "carnivalesque" he seems to be referring to Mikhail Bakhtín, suggesting that there are floating borders between the performer and the audience, and to the cultural theorist Sue Vic who believes that "the whole point of carnival . . . is that the viewer is also a participant" (Laing 2004:7). What he means by "Dionysian" he does not reveal, but it could be the concept that he, together with the anarchist writer Hakim Bey Bey quickly introduces as – TAZ ("Temporary Autonomous Zone"), further developed and conceptualized by James Ingham:

> Incorporating a quotation from Hillegonda Rietveld (Rietveld 1993) Ingham writes that TAZ is "a useful analytical concept that

> allows us to acknowledge that virtual sound worlds can bring people together in fluid associations driven by desire and imagination in which music can function 'to pump a desire into human bodies to move, to dance and let go'."
>
> (Ingham 1999:112, Laing 2004:7)

At Roskilde

But surely it was this yearning to "pump a desire into human bodies to move, to dance and let go," that became the main motivation for the rock festival in Roskilde. Folk singer Andrew John, who was a member of the festival's management team, says that the festival initiator Carl Fischer was clearly inspired by the *Woodstock* movie, while Andrew John himself was on the Isle of Wight in '69 with Bob Dylan, The Who and The Band (Rung 1995:20). But if the inspiration was purely usurping from already mythological festivals, the organizers' handling of this, according to one of the volunteers, Jan Degner, seems murkier:

> The actual organizers of the first Roskilde Festival in 1971 were a few idealistic but naive high school students in Roskilde, whom Carl Fischer got to apply for all the permits, enter into agreements with local suppliers and helped practically to build and run the festival. But it was these young people who were left to pay the bills.
>
> (Rung 1995:26–27)

Nevertheless, this first festival turned out to be so noteworthy that it appealed to both new promoters and to the Roskilde Municipality. This becomes apparent with convincing clarity through the many contributions to the Roskilde Museum's 25th Roskilde Festival anniversary festival book. It is also apparent that from the very beginning that support of the festival was a must for the city's leading politicians and civil servants, despite the fact that other politicians and some voters were fervently against it.

Already in his introduction to the festival book, Mayor Henrik Christiansen discusses the dissonant murmurings from many citizens, but then immediately adds:

> These murmurings have, however, dissipated over the years, probably for three reasons: the intense preparation and planning strategy from the festival management's side, the Roskilde Foundation's support for working with young people, plus, for many organizations, it was a chance to earn money via voluntary work

> while the festival is going on. . . . The city again becomes that spot on the Danish map that all young people are drawn to. Roskilde is the place many young foreigners identify Denmark with.
>
> (Rung 1995:6)

In 1995, functioning as both co-director and co-festival coordinator, spokesperson Leif Skov adopts a more global perspective in his list of the Roskilde Festival's international predecessors, albeit not in chronological order – "The Newport Festival (jazz festival, USA), Woodstock (USA), Altamount (USA) and the Isle of Wight (England)" (Rung 1995:7). Looking back at the 25 years, he notes with satisfaction

> that real commercial rock music festivals, with size, meaning and many years behind them, are not to be found anywhere in the world – surviving festivals have other primary goals rather than just financial gain. A nice law of nature to be able to apply to a cultural area.
>
> (Rung 1995:9)

In Leif Skov's rear-view mirror, the festival's first year looks rather meager: happenstance prevailed, musically, one was offered a little bit of everything ("folk, jazz, rock, pop, etc."), there was poor audience service and jacked up beer & water prices. The fact that the festival survived at all "that first fragile year" was due solely to "the freedom and the attitude of the people involved." But toward the end of the 1970s the festival management began to

> think in a more forward looking manner, about profile, service, quality, work and organizational structures, respecting the audience more than earnings . . ., and in the first years of the 1980s, the musical line-up continued to make the Roskilde Festival the leading forward-looking festival in the world for rhythmic music and – especially – for the musical expression of youth culture.
>
> Through a large part of Roskilde Festival's 25 year history style changes or adjustments have given rise to frustrations and disappointment. The festival currently does not have a folk music stage, nor a jazz stage, nor an amateur stage. When these stages disappeared, the representatives of these genres took care of business and protested, looking after their own interests, while the festival, also looking after its own interests, developed a narrower,

> contemporary and more weighty profile – the same profile that has garnered the festival its great recognition – from virtually every point of view. The Roskilde Festival dares, wants, and is able to do something that no one – or few – others dare, want or are able to do.
>
> (Rung 1995:9–10)

Leif Skov's 25th anniversary contribution is not a eulogy, but a celebratory speech. And yet, he builds it up in exactly the same way as Pericles did 2426 years earlier, with his simultaneously admonishing and forward looking programming words (see pages 11 and 72). Skov emphasizes the festival's development from a loosely structured and relatively poor quality presentation to an effective, tightly trimmed organization. He praises the festival's achieved recognition, high regard, and international fame. He delimits and clearly characterizes the festivals opponents and their weaknesses, and emphasizes the vision of the festival leadership and their vigor – to say nothing of their strength and daring.

Leif Skov wants to respond to those critics who must, of course, be there, and were there throughout the 80s and 90s. But he also wants to present his organization, his festival service, and his music strategy to the public consciousness as absolutely and indisputably superior:

> The Roskilde Festival is today an attractive music festival. It takes place in Roskilde, Denmark, but is no longer a local or a national event. It has been established and recognized as more than that across all borders. Some call the festival an "annually returning international cultural political manifestation," the Nordic Council of Ministers appointed it as a "Nordic Culture Festival" and 3 weeks before the anniversary celebration in 1995, the Danish postal service published a stamp with the festival's trademark (the orange canopy/stage cover) as motif. Thus the event and the phenomenon were immortalized.
>
> (Rung 1995:11)

This text gives one an impression of a strong leader and a significant personality. His presentation of the range of problems with subsequent clarifications and correct solutions creates full confidence in his future strategies and organizational approaches. At each end of 2,426 years, the festival coordinator and the statesman speak with one voice.

The Roskilde Foundation

The idea of letting the Roskilde Foundation enter into the festival economy arose with Vice Commissioner Niels Borchersen, who in 1971 was responsible for renting and supervising the livestock fairgrounds. He had closely followed the festival with its 10,000 participants (3,000 crawled through the fence and failed to pay) and had a full official overview of its economic potential. He went to his chief municipal director, Henning Jaquet, and presented him with the situation:

> There is really a lot of money in circulation at such an event, and we ought to somehow ensure that this money doesn't go to Copenhagen or anywhere else, but stays in Roskilde. We talked back and forth, and the idea arose to establish the Roskilde Foundation as the organizer of future events.
>
> (Rung 1995:19)

Realization of this idea was actually within reach. Borchersen's chief, Henning Jaquet, was the chairman of the Roskilde Foundation. This association arranged Roskilde's annual city festivals and made sure that profits from these events went to children and youth work in Roskilde. The chairman/municipal director then asked the head of the Roskilde Youth Club, and member of the Roskilde Foundation's business committee, Erik Larsen, together with another business committee member, to contact the American folk singer, Tony Busch, who had approached Borchersen about putting on a festival in the summer of 1972.

The Roskilde Foundation thus takes over the festival – not only in terms of legal and economic issues and logistics, but also the music. All based on the idea as formulated by Niels Borchersen, that there is a lot of money in circulation and it should go to good purposes in Roskilde. But even though the Roskilde Foundation now seems to be the actual festival organizer, it was implemented by the foundation's General Assembly as a "beat festival on 'the New Livestock Fairgrounds'" that is a cooperative contract between Tony Busch and the Roskilde Foundation, administered by Erik Larsen:

> At the Roskilde Foundation's Business Committee meeting on December 3, 1971, I presented a proposal for a festival in June 1972 in collaboration with Tony Busch. According to the proposal, half of the profits would go to the Roskilde Foundation and half to

> Tony Busch. The Roskilde Foundation would have all rights on the grounds for sale of food, drinks etc., but must guarantee the municipality DKK 50,000 to cover potential damage to the site.
>
> [The contract] was drawn up with Tony Busch (who distributed risk/dividends to Tony Busch's limited company "Kaunos" and to the Roskilde Foundation), with final clarification by the Roskilde Municipality regarding all claims, police, fire chief, building inspectors, etc. as well as the Agricultural Association because of their relationship with the Livestock Fairgrounds.
>
> (Rung 1995:30–31)

As can be seen from Erik Larsen's quoted presentation about any processing issues and gaining approval, the municipality's and the Roskilde Foundation's control of the festival is tangible. And there is no concealment of motive in chairman and municipal director Jaquet's report in April 1972, in which he elegantly succeeds in switching hats between his association and the municipality:

> The Business Committee has approved that the Roskilde Foundation joins the event of this year's beat festival at the New Livestock Fairgrounds. . . . It is not without reservations that the Executive Committee agrees to this event, but if it is successful, we should be able to secure a nice return for the Roskilde Foundation's work.
>
> (Rung 1995:32)

Which is precisely what happened in 1972, and all the following years. While *association chairman* Jaquet firmly eyed the profits that the festival put in the association's box for the benefit of working with local youth, *municipal director* Jaquet and other committee members had to deal with criticism, epithets and provocations from angry politicians and citizens who were outraged that the foundation could "arrange such a pigsty here in the city" (Rung 1995:34).

Volunteer at the earlier festivals Jan Degner recalls that Inge Krogh, the Christian People's Party Member of Parliament, in 1976 criticized the lifestyle among the participants (Rung 1995:23): "Even more absurd was the politician Erhard Jacobsen's accusations in 1978 against Denmark's Radio's coverage of the festival. Erhard believed that DR employees cultivated party-political interests and at the same time he called the festival a pseudo-event" (Rung 1995:28).

From the beginning, the Roskilde Festival and the Roskilde Municipality opposed the Christian and populist politicians and their constituency. The Christian People's Party was founded in 1970 in protest against the abolishment the year before of a ban on image pornography (see *Danish Women's Biographical Encyclopedia* 2000) and abortion legislation that had been liberalized that same year. For Inge Krogh, a fanatic opponent of these new laws, believed the Roskilde Festival represented "living pornography" – even worse than porn clubs and massage clinics. Inge Krogh personally visited a number of sites, which, in her opinion, were in moral dissolution, also including the Roskilde Festival, where she was photographed debating with two bare-breasted young women (Rung 1995:23).

For Erhard Jacobsen, the founder of the Center Democratic Party in 1973, the naked look was hardly a stumbling block. On the other hand, for him the problem was the festival phenomenon itself; he considered it to be an incubatory for left-wing indoctrination of youth.

This Christian populist criticism, however, bounced right off the festival leadership, which was anchored not only in Roskilde Municipality's political majority, but also beyond. Here, they were completely comfortable with the agreed upon management structure. Roskilde's municipal democracy could accommodate the festival's temporary deviations from moral and behavioral norms, as well as certain exemptions from the covenant with the police.

The police

The "city-state" of Roskilde consists of a politically led municipality, a powerful local foundation with the goal of providing the city's young people with a good upbringing and environment, a bishop authority and the police.

The festival guests did not want a police presence in 1971. This is why they failed to carry out the statutory inspections in that year. A number of parents' inquiries about the intake of alcohol and drugs led to the deployment of a civil police in 1972, but the arrests that were made generated violent protests and counter-attacks precisely because of the police's "civil disguise." Starting in 1973, it was decided to supply uniformed police in the hope that the festival participants would perceive it as part of the area's normal scene. However, this attitude took a few years before it was accepted. Many festival participants' "outdoor" knowledge of the police originated from protests against the Vietnam War or from the housing demonstrations that were taking place at that time, and Vice Police Director Niels Bonde had to admit that the experiment needed a roll-out period:

> The first year [1973], the uniformed police were met with various forms of harassment, but surprisingly quickly, the police were

> accepted as a natural part of the scene and a security-creating element for young people who were interested in the music, but for many, a little afraid of the drugs and violence.
>
> (Rung 1995:39)

It should be noted, however, that the presence of a civilian crew of especially "festival-dressed" police was maintained – at least until the 1990s (according to a source in the Copenhagen Police).

That the assimilation took place so quickly was due to the fact that the police authority accepted a special "inside-the-fence" decree, that in part freed the police up to ignore drunkenness (alcohol or narcotics) that was not considered offensive to others, and in part shifted some activities to a special Samaritan guard, whenever needed. Neither was enforcement of "indecent exposure," "lasciviousness," or the "indecency clause" considered part of police duties. Only fights, violence, rape and drug sales (and after 2000 also moshing and crowd surfing) were prohibited.

The "city-state" of Roskilde's targeted, preventive drug efforts and its liberal handling of the use of intoxicants in the festival area, that is to say "inside-the-fence," solved a number of problems all at once. Yes, one could say that the "city-state" introduced a local statute whose purpose was to secure the festival as a legal liberated space. This came about through the introduction of a police presence so large that the force had to be recruited from the entire Greater Copenhagen region.

The joy and relaxation that permeates the festival is due to this "liberated space contract." That the well-defined transgressions and violations of laws and regulations that are applicable "outside-the-fence" don't apply "inside-the-fence."

The canopy symbol

The Roskilde Festival logo and symbol since 1978 has been and remains the orange canopy tent – The Orange Stage. Festival coordinator Leif Skov "spotted" the tent in a photo in the English rock weekly *Express* in the summer of 1977, where the band Queen played in Hyde Park. The tent was originally built for the Rolling Stones, which had toured with it in Europe in 1976. After several inquiries, Skov found out who owned the canopy, which, moreover, was complicated by the fact that The Stones, as was customary, had set up an independent firm for the maintenance and renting of the tent. This company was now bankrupt, and as few bands wanted to appear in Rolling Stone's abandoned "robes," the canopy was thus for sale.

Leif Skov located the remains of the tent, which was being held back in a farm building by a truck driver who was owed money by the bankrupt company. He describes visiting the truck driver's farm as a pilgrimage and describes in minute detail what must have been a revelation to his eyes:

> It was supposed to be inside an old, rusty and hollow corrugated tin hangar. And what a sight. A fascinating rock 'n' roll graveyard for things that Shirley [the trucker] had hauled around for rock legends. Here were huge floodlights that Pink Floyd had used at the Pompeii concerts – and the construction for Queen's stage, shaped like a giant queen's crown with hundreds of lamps like pearls and diamonds. Also the orange PVC cloth for the Rolling Stone's orange canopy was there. Everything seemed to have just been unloaded and thrown in there.
>
> (Rung 1995:115–116)

The canopy was brought to Denmark with DFDS Seaways, fully restored to its original extent and put into use during the summer of 1978. In 1983, the worn PVC cloth was replaced with new material and also got a structural facelift:

> In 1995, the Canopy in Roskilde was used for the 18th time – 6 times in the old version, 12 times in the new. The Canopy is the festival's logo – and symbol of its development. In 1995, just as distinctive and beautiful as it was in 1978.
>
> (Rung 1995:117)

The Orange Stage is erected and taken down by a special team of volunteers.

> The small, cool, devoted group, who over the years formed the "Canopy Crew" consisted of 15–20 volunteers who live in the festival area for 2–3 weeks to raise the canopy and its surroundings – and then pack it all down again – and who sometimes meet between two festivals to work weekends to maintain the 3–4 tons of canopy and metal.
>
> (Rung 1995:119)

The word "canopy" has many meanings. Some of them are "roof, tent or structure," "parachute," "wireless broadband solutions," and a "canopy over an altar or throne – that is to say an authority symbol." Leif Skov himself was a member of the Canopy Crew 1978–1988.

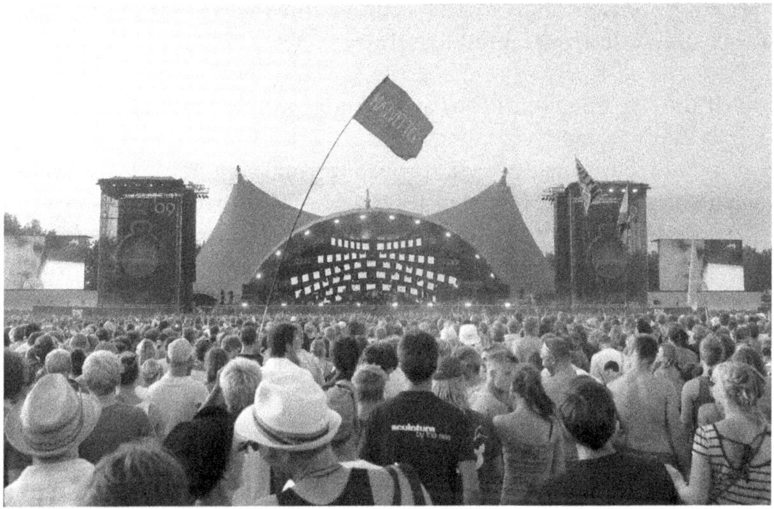

Figure 4.2 The Orange Stage

Source: Photo by Anders Graver

Just as Pericles completed the decoration of the Acropolis with a frieze and the Pallas Athena statue of gold and ivory, Leif Skov restored the Rolling Stones' canopy tent and resurrected it as the festival symbol: The Orange Stage (Figure 4.1).

Organization and economy

In 2009, Denmark's official tourism organization VisitDenmark, in collaboration with three other Danish tourism organizations and the Roskilde Festival, published a study *The Festival as Tourist Magnet – An Economic Tourism Study of Denmark's Largest Culture Festival 08*, which mapped out, for that particular year's festival, where the participants came from, in Denmark, the Nordic countries and other countries as well. The study looked at where participants spent the night, how big their individual festival budgets were, as well as their age and how often they participated in the festival. The study offered no surprises. It profiled the average participant as a 25-year-old male Copenhagener, who spent the night in the camping area, spent DKK 4,700 during the festival's eight days (including the entrance fee of DKK 1,650), and participated in the festival six times before. As to why it was not female Copenhageners who topped the list or even that the gender of attendees didn't split fifty-fifty, the Danish newspaper journalist Dorte Hygum Sørensen after a conversation with the festival's spokesman Esben Danielsen, explained like this:

> If the hygiene conditions at Roskilde were better, there might be as many women as male guests. . . . Rock festivals are the kind of events that cause people to push normal boundaries. But where men have no problems using the festival's surrounding fences as toilets – even if the fences are neighbors to food stalls – women obviously prefer to lock the door behind them in a room containing something as civilized as toilet paper.
>
> (Hygum Sørensen: Politiken 7 February 2009)

Former spokesman and development manager Esben Danielsen, however, questioned VisitDenmark's analysis, which is based on just 800 respondents. The festival's own and far larger analyses show only a small variance, with a few percent more men than women. And "in the summer of 2011, the gender distribution was 50–50" (Danielsen tells me in a note 6 November 2011).

The study's other audience analyses which for 2008 determined declining foreign participation and increasing Danish, could, if desired, be explained by taking stock of other European rock festivals; not least of which is the fact that the many English festivals each year are completely sold out, that the Ringe Festival on the island of Fyn had ceased, as did the Hultsfred Festival in Southern Sweden, plus the study clearly states that festivals are also subject to prevailing market mechanisms. In this respect, the VisitDenmark study was quite predictable.

That was also the case with regard to the Roskilde Festival's economic relation to the "city state" of Roskilde. It had been recognized for decades that the festival contributes to the city's tourism revenue. This is also the conclusion of the VisitDenmark study – which, however, spokesman Esben Danielsen (Hygum Sørensen: Politiken 7 February 2009) wisely chooses to be surprised by. During future negotiations with the "city state" he and the rest of the management could rely on the study's main conclusion:

> Audience, volunteers and media people at Roskilde Festival generated 384 million Danish crowns in direct tourism revenue in Denmark and is thus decisive for Roskilde's total tourism economy, where the festival corresponds to one fourth to one-third of the annual revenue. From this revenue, the festival brought in

> more than 113 million crowns to Denmark from direct foreign consumption. . . .
>
> The festival generated over six tourist overnights per participant during the festival, but also in the vicinity of 100,000 other overnights before and after the festival, for a total value of at least 50 million DKK.
>
> (VisitDenmark 2009:3)

The importance of the festival for the "city-state" of Roskilde can hardly be overestimated. In addition, the festival management is an active partner in the city's cultural, educational, and business life – most recently as a significant stakeholder in the new innovative district Musicon, with a folk high school, vocational schools, technical schools, artistic and gastronomic workshops, greenhouses for entrepreneurs, a rock museum, housing and much more.

The music

Instruments and gear

For the most, rock music is not performed on instruments used by classical symphony orchestras or classical jazz bands. First came the blues and country music, then 1950s rock 'n' roll, followed by1960s beat music, all of which paved the way for the instruments, sound, light technology and industry that today is an integral part of any rock festival economy.

During the 1960s, rock was defined as "electric music." Electrical amplification raised the sound level to such an extent that four to six musicians and singers could outdo even the largest symphony orchestra as far as the decibel level is concerned. But more important was the sound quality, specifically the guitar's many sound and distortion possibilities. The guitar became rock music's "brand" – visualized by Jimi Hendrix (see Figure 4.3), who during his last years completed concerts by igniting his instrument so that it appeared in luminous flames.

Like Greek antiquity's double-auloi, the guitar is both genre identifier and visual symbol, as well as a communicative resource. Whether defining the instrument as a lead, rhythm, or bass guitar, the electric guitar is the genre's most specific expression. The literary and cultural historian Perry Meisel puts the "guitar genre" into historical and philosophical context in his book *The Myth of Popular Culture from Dante to Dylan* (2010), where in a critical analysis of Theodor W. Adorno's jazz

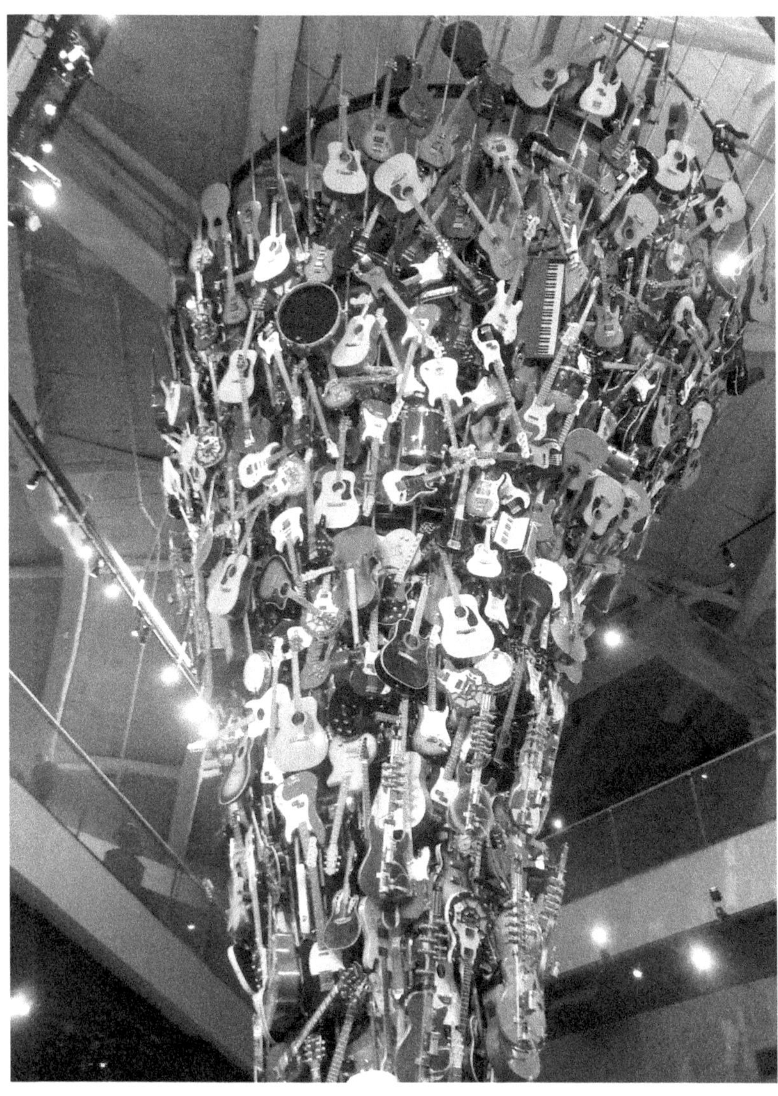

Figure 4.3 Like a glittering totem pole, this 10 meter high guitar sculpture towers over the central galleries in Seattle's Museum of Pop Culture (MoPOP). Initially inspired by Jimi Hendrix, the museum has continued to evolve since opening in 2000 to incorporate popular music, science fiction, fantasy, horror, video games, fashion, film, literature, and other aspects of popular culture. (Artist: Trimpin. Courtesy of the Museum of Pop Culture, Seattle, WA)

Source: Photo by MoPop, Seattle

criticism, he demonstrates that the same dialectic wave is generated in so-called popular music that Adorno claims only for classically composed music:

> In pop music, the dialectical dynamic is the call-and-response of generations of musicians over time, in jazz, urban blues, folk music, and rock and roll, as each new wave sweeps away the one before it. How wrong Adorno is. Within the real cosmogony of jazz, be-bop dialectically overturns swing in a different way – by electrifying it to frustrate our assumptions about what is "natural" and what is not. The scrim here is the mythology of authentic black rural or "folk" culture against which the shrewd Muddy Waters trades upon his arrival in Chicago from the Delta. This moment constitutes the epistemological break that rock and roll is in cultural history. With electrical guitar, it completes the philosophical work that begins with Dante.
>
> (Meisel 2010:xi)

Adorno hardly came to obstruct the artistic or audience progression of beat and rock music in Europe or on the world stage. Living in Frankfurt, he probably had heard of the Isle of Wight Festival in 1968. Woodstock took place in 1969 from 15–18 August, a week after Adorno's death. Thus, he came to be acquainted with hippie and 68 culture.

The program

In 1971, The Roskilde Festival program offered music from 33 bands, six of which came from England and two from the USA. Among the remaining 25 were 13 rock bands and 12 folk/blues/jazz bands. Thus, festival participants encountered a small number of English and American bands, but the music was dominated by Danish groups such as Alrune Rod, Burnin Red Ivanhoe, Gasolin and Dr. Dopo Jam, flanked by that era's leading traditional jazz orchestras like Papa Bue, Lousiana Hot Seven, Fessor's Big City Band, Delta Blues Band and the folk singers Caesar, Per Dich, Poul Dissing and Sebastian (see Roskilde Festival's website: History: Bands ff.).

This genre-breakdown continued until the end of the 1970s, when rock partly replaced other genres, and partly split into "many juxtaposed musical styles, each of which permeated the media with its music, clothing, attitudes and lifestyle" (Reinholdt Nielsen 2003:98). In 1972, 32 bands played the festival with many of the same names from before. Fessor's Big City Band was the only revival jazz representative. On the other hand, the English rock band The Kinks was on the stage.

The offerings are consolidated into 23 bands in 1973, including reprises from Alrune Rod, Burnin Red Ivanhoe, Gasolin, Fessor's Big City Band – supplemented by Jørgen Olsen, Red Mother, the Greenlandic group Sume, the revival jazz band the Kansas City Stompers and folk musician Evald Thomsen & the Spillemænd (Fiddlers). In contrast, in 1974 the program would be expanded to 38 bands with groups such as Savage Rose, Secret Oyster, East Jutland Music Supply and Papa Benny's Jazz Men.

The development and politics continued in this way right on up through the decade. There was room for established and newer Danish rock bands at the festival, flanked by foreign stars – Ravi Shankar, Procol Harum, Dr. Hook, Weather Report, Björn Afzelius, Elvis Costello, Taj Mahal, Dollar Brand, Tania Maria, the Brecker Brothers, Jan Hammarlund, and the Red Hot Chili Peppers. Among the returning Danish bands there was also room for up and coming bands throughout the 70s – Bifrost, Ache, Entrance, C.V. Jørgensen, Cox Orange, Shit & Chanel, Jomfru Ane Band, the Skousen/Ingeman/Stig Møller Band and the Anne Linnet Band. In 1980, almost 60 bands played the festival.

Interesting is that revival jazz's rich representation at Roskilde ends with Papa Bue's concert in 1976. Up until this point, this style of jazz had been an important brand and a great attraction for the festival. Revival jazz, which came to Denmark in the late 1950s, had set itself so firmly in the young Danish firmament that neither The Beatles, The Rolling Stones, The Kinks nor the many Danish rock groups were able to displace it. But from 1977 revival jazz was displaced by the swing orchestra Leonardo Pedersen's Jazz Chapel and then the following year the festival freed itself from the older jazz style completely in order to, in 1979 and 1980, be able to present modern jazz with Denmark's Radio Big Band, Thad Jones and the "almost big band" Eclipse.

With the jazz program, the festival attracted and maintained much of its original younger revival audience but, over a five-six-year period, transformed this into (from a harmonic point of view) a stable rock audience and, for every passing year, "upgraded it" to a more free and experimental kind of rock, which became the festival's musical hallmark in the 1980s.

In Denmark, as in England, movement toward producing music for an essentially rock audience was a must. The American revival wave especially hit these two European countries with their large generations born between 1943 and 1947. Rock could not be taken in unintegrated or untransformed. In 1979, however, this process seemed so advanced that the festival could invite modern jazz harmonies onto the festival stages as a kind of stabilizing corrective or supplement to the experimental rock. Modern jazz had easily merged with several rock styles and not so few musicians cultivated these forms. In addition, several jazz musicians finally left jazz behind in favor of rock: Karsten Vogel (Burnin Red Ivanhoe), Franz Beckerlee (Gasolin), Peter Ingemann (Red Mother, Skousen & Ingemann).

In the first five years of the 1980s, the number of bands performing at Roskilde was 55–60, with one third being international (that is to say, non-Nordic). The Danish rock scene was still well represented, but from 1986 the number of foreign (non-Nordic) groups expanded to over half of the participating bands, which all together reached 75 in 1989 (with 40 foreign bands). This was not only due to the growth in the number of American and English bands, but also an increased access to world music bands. The festival management moved steadily toward the forward-looking jazz and folk-free scene, that since has become the expression of the festival's youth culture.

Nevertheless, jazz still characterized the 1980s festival concert programs, where the genre was represented every year by groups such as the Ole Molins Trio (1981), Pierre Dørge and the New Jungle Orchestra, the Oregon City Jazz Band (1983) Trille with Band (1984), Povl Dissing, Benny Andersen, Jens Jefsen (1985 and 1988), Mikkelborg/Knudsen/Niels-Henning Ørsted Pedersen (1987), Bo Stief Five (1988), Bazar, Marylin Mazur (1989). On the other hand, there is a sharp reduction in known Danish rock bands – for example, in 1989 they were replaced by Hanne Boel, Thomas Helmig, C.V. Jørgensen and Poul Krebs.

In the 1990s, the audience continued to grow, peaking through the 25th anniversary in 1995 with 90,000 participants (1994–1997). The number of concerts surpassed 150 and the proportion of foreign bands grew to more than two-thirds. The program became international, dominated by English and American names, but groups from all over Europe and the world were welcomed as well. Every year the festival recruited big names, several of which were acclaimed returnees: Bob Dylan (1990, 1995, 1998), Elvis Costello (1991, 1994, 1995), Marianne Faithfull, Paul Simon (1991), Pearl Jam (1992, 2000), Björk (1994), David Bowie, Red Hot Chili Peppers and the Sex Pistols (1996), Phish, Radiohead (1997), Metallica, REM, Robbie Williams (1999), Lou Reed and as mentioned Pearl Jam (2000).

As for Danish bands in the 1990s, fewer and fewer played the festival and even fewer of the most well known gave more than two concerts in the decade: D.A.D. 6 concerts, Dizzy Mizz Lizzy 4, Lars H.U.G. and C.V. Jørgensen 3, while Malurt, Miss B. Haven, TV-2, Sort Sol, Henning Stærk, Hanne Boel, Dicte and Johnny Madsen each were at Roskilde just twice during that decade. This policy changed and programming increasingly valued domestic music as an area of growth: At the festival in 2000, over 50 of the 90s' newer Danish bands participated. Among others: Nephew.

Thus, there can be no doubt that during the 1990s the festival management sought to create a musical "canon" that would retain former festival participants and recruit new ones. With Dylan and Costello as permanent backdrops – Dylan as a living connection back to the Isle of Wight and Woodstock – the festival cemented its international heritage while at the same time prioritized and continuously evaluated and valued Danish rock culture and art in regard for the diverse audience.

After the accident during the Pearl Jam concert at the Orange Stage, where nine festival participants died from lack of oxygen in front of the stage, there was a reassessment of the 90's canon

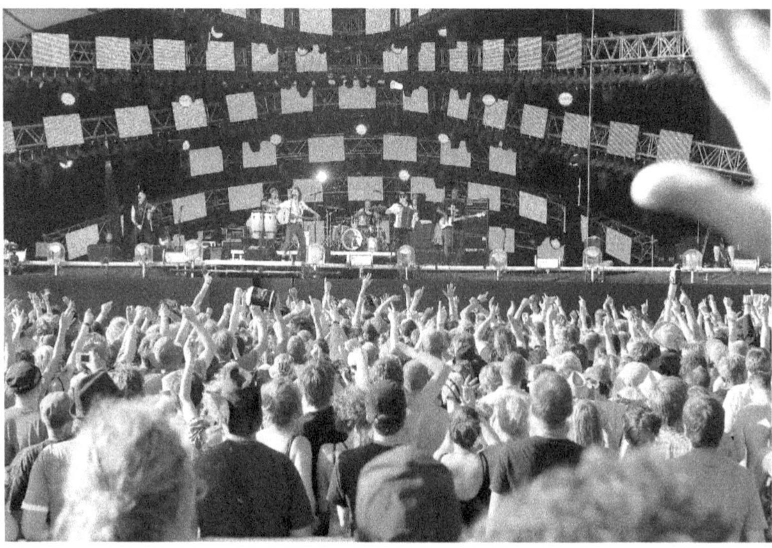

Figure 4.4 Gogol Bordello, The Orange Stage 2009

Source: Photo by Anders Graver

(in addition to a very extensive and costly security effort). 100,000 festival participants showed up for a fully reconceived concept, which in its full international and national scope not only embraced the "musical expression of youth culture," as the festival director Leif Skov formulated it (Rung 1995:9), but also presented the classic canon internationally as well as nationally :

Bob Dylan
Elvis Costello
R.E.M.
Mikael Wiehe

D.A.D.
Dizzy Mizz Lizzy
Thomas Helmig
C. V. Jørgensen
Johnny Madsen
Bo Stief
Sume

This canon (see Figure 4.5) continued through the decade, but at the same time reflected the growing difficulty of honoring internationally renowned bands and their burgeoning economic demands. While the concert totals showed great genre and global variety regarding established bands and grass roots, the selective festival programming presented a stable international and national canon:

Thus the Roskilde Festival's music program runs on two tracks – a development track that incorporates new genres, new subcultures and new technical (and technological) expressions, tests them then perhaps embraces some of them for shorter or longer periods. And a canon track that maintains the Dylan-era and Danish 70s tone with Savage Rose, C.V. Jørgensen and Niels Skousen.

In the first part of the following decade 2011–2015, canonical recycling decreased, however, some bands were re-presented each year: Björk in 2012, Metallica in 2013, Trentemøller in 2014 and Mew in 2015. By contrast, approximately every two years a world class act was part of the program: Bruce Springsteen in 2012, The Rolling Stones in 2014, and Paul McCartney in 2015. Bob Dylan was the festival star in 2019.

Rock's evolution from the Isle of Wight and Woodstock in the late 1960s up through today reflects a musical, technological, and

One concert
Two concerts
Three concerts
Four concerts

	National	International
2001	D-A-D Dizzy Mizz Lizzy Thomas Helmig C.V. Jørgensen	Bob Dylan Elvis Costello R.E.M.
2002	Thomas Helmig C.V. Jørgensen The Raveonettes Niels Skousen Band The Savage Rose	Red Hot Chili Peppers
2003	Kashmir Lars H.U.G. Mew The Raveonettes	Björk Metallica
2004	Nephew	Santana
2005	D-A-D. Mew The Raveonettes	Duran Duran
2006	Kashmir	Bob Dylan
2007	Nephew	Björk Red Hot Chili Peppers The Who
2008	The Raveonettes	Nick Cave Radiohead Neil Young
2009	Mew Trentemøller	Nick Cave
2010	Nephew C.V. Jørgensen Dizzy Mizz Lizzy Kashmir	Prince

Figure 4.5 The concert canon 2001–2010

economic development. Per Reinholdt Nielsen summarizes this development from a media group perspective:

> If rock in the 1950s arose locally around the United States on a lot of small record companies, the big companies like CBS, EMI,

> Capitol, MCA, Polygram, RCA, A&M and Warner now embraced rock for themselves. They followed the movements of the music closely and signed contracts with all new names. All companies were large media companies, several of them with interests in TV, film, literature, news media and music. They bought up the most lucrative smaller record labels. Concurrently with the growing record sales that peaked in 1977–78, the concert industry expanded as well. With new P.A. installations, which moved the speakers forward in front of the band, and with their increased decibel levels, performers could play far larger halls and stadiums as well. Rock musicians could now appear for thousands of people.
>
> (Reinholdt Nielsen 2003:101)

Nude culture

The great liberation

Booze, drugs, and sex fill newspaper articles and accounts of festival experiences (Rung 1995, Jensen 2003). What one might call the "festival essence" is formulated without judgment or sentimentality in Dave White's previously cited characteristics of the "Woodstock-society" in 1969:

> Largely undaunted, attendees happily shared their food, drugs, booze and sexual partners with those who were without, and frolicked in the mud.
>
> (White: Homepage, Woodstock 101)

The 2010 edition of the Roskilde Festival is discussed in an interview in the Danish newspaper *Politiken* with Kristine Munkgård Pedersen (2010), the author of a PhD thesis about the festival:

> The festival manages . . . to offer young people a space where one can truly get wild and crazy and do all these potentially immoral things like whoring, drinking and getting filthy.

The festival's exquisite sensuality is driven, it seems, by alcohol, drugs, free sex, nudity and mud. Most of these ingredients can be experienced or consumed – albeit not all legally – in the community beyond the festival fences, except for two: nudity and mud.

In her PhD thesis, Kristine Munkgård Pedersen, focuses on the "liminal space" that this liberated behavior is played out in, referring to Victor Turner's analysis of ritual:

> In many ways the Roskilde Festival's culture is characterized by the festival's long duration, which to a high degree demands its audience. Primitive living conditions, long nights and high alcohol consumption are a demanding cocktail that embodies the festival's socio-material aesthetics and symbolism. Intense and disgusting elements that are not allowed in other contexts are, at the festival, socially acceptable or even the norm. It is in this liminality that the unique community of festival culture thrives, a community that can best be described by Victor Turner's ritual concept of "communitas."
>
> (Turner 1969)

It is the desire to achieve this all-encompassing ritual community that drives the festival-goer into this liminality's unpredictable state of happiness.

Orgies

During ancient Greek Dionysian feasts, nudity was not only part of the orgies and night parties in the streets, but also extended to the sports competitions. The naked sportsmen smeared themselves in a mixture of mud and dust and olive oil so as not to dehydrate during matches and competitions. As previously mentioned, the human body as portrayed in sculptures, reliefs, and drawings were most often naked.

The orgy itself is referred to either in connection with cultic gatherings (the cult of Dionysus in the mountains) or mythological stories (wedding parties that evolved into sex orgies). But otherwise, one must "assume" that actual orgies took place within the highly heralded private life of Pericles and other statesmen – that is to say, by agreement and with consent of the parties involved, whether voluntary, desired or paid.

This is the same today. Most orgies take place away from the public eye, but publicity or documentation of some examples sometimes slip out to the media. Thus, the Italian Prime Minister Silvio Berlusconi's orgy on 19 September 2009:

> The newspaper *La Republica* published . . . descriptions of what happened on September 19 in Berlusconi's villa San Martino near Milan.

> According to intercepted telephone calls and witness reports, Berlusconi spent the evening with two men and up to 25 young women. . . . After dinner, the women decamped to what two of them refer to as the "bunga-bunga room," which was equipped like a nightclub with a stripper bar.
>
> "Bunga-bunga," according to the investigative authority, refers to orgies. The women changed to nursing or police uniforms and, topless, took part in a strip competition where they simulated having sex. The one who gave the best performance was chosen to stay overnight.
>
> (*Politiken*, Danish newspaper 17.1.2011)

We also have orgies in Denmark. At Aalborg University there is a video recording of a cultic orgy held in a security room in the university's basement. The recording shows a

> sex orgy with at least four men and one woman at Aalborg University. A university professor organized . . . several orgies. The sexual encounters were rather advanced and several orgies were held at the university. [The four men were] dressed in monk frocks while performing hour-long sex with a woman. Apparently everyone participated voluntarily . . . and various instruments were used during the sexual act. The act itself was carefully planned.
>
> (*BT*, Danish newspaper 10.12.2010)

Public knowledge of these orgies usually only come about if there has been illegalities: for Berlusconi, this was due to the involvement of a woman who was under the age of sexual consent in Italy; at Aalborg University, the orgy became public due to improper use of public property for private purposes.

In the Italian example, the legal system was involved. Not so in the Aalborg case, where the professor, after a reprimand from the chancellor for abuse of the university's building resources, could continue to hold sex orgies in private or on rented premises with cult members recruited from the Internet.

Mud wrestling and the Naked Race

Sex orgies have always been with us, but public visibility of these orgies is connected to the morality of a particular era. The early rock festivals, from the late 1960s and up through the 1970s are all associated with hippie culture's group sex, partner exchanges and nudity. From the start, nudity became a strong festival brand.

Not on the stage itself. In 1976, Dr. Hook appeared as the first naked band (Rung 1995:124, Jensen 2003:110), and nude culture quickly acquired its symbols and rituals. The best known are the Naked Race and mud wrestling, which take place every year. But also, an installation like the "Tower of Butts" from 1987 (see Figure 4.6) shows that the "naked look" continued beyond the 1970s. Mud wrestling isn't initiated or organized by the festival management. It spontaneously takes place throughout the festival and is one of the most popular activities. Naked or half-naked wrestling in mud pools or basins has great power to fascinate – judging by the large amount of photos and videos posted on the world's websites. Certainly, the erotic connotations exposed during the wrestling are not hidden Mud wrestling follows Richard Schechner's schematics of a sudden event or "Eruption" and a planned event or "Procession" (Schechner 1988:177–178). The former occurs because two people decide to wrestle in a random mud pool, a passing audience stops to look on. Thus, the mud wrestlers become performers and creators of a "hot event," or an "eruption." The audience can choose themselves how close or distant they want to be from the performers. They can also choose to participate and thus become performers themselves. In a planned event in an "authorized" mud pool or mud basin, performers and audiences are clearly delineated and defined, and perhaps even led or invited to the experience ("procession"). The performers appear in pairs and in an agreed order, and the audience does not usually interact in the fight. This is a performance, as the many videos clearly document.

Mud wrestling at the Roskilde Festival has the same high status as wrestling matches had in ancient Greek festivals and sporting contests, and a winner is lifted up to glory and honor, as can be seen on the cover photo of Erik Jensen's book *At Roskilde*, which can easily be compared to the golden sculpture of Athens goddess Pallas Athene in the Parthenon temple at the Acropolis (see Figures 4.7 and 4.8).

The Naked Race (see Figure 4.9) is the second major interactive nude attraction at the Roskilde Festival. But even though the Naked Race today is an institution at the festival, it is neither tradition nor play, but rather ritual and a marker. The unisex competition, which chooses a winner from each gender, is a new addition to the communicative and intellectual aspect of the festival's 50-year history:

> The first official edition of the naked race dates back to Saturday, June 27, 1998, when seven men and one woman participated. It

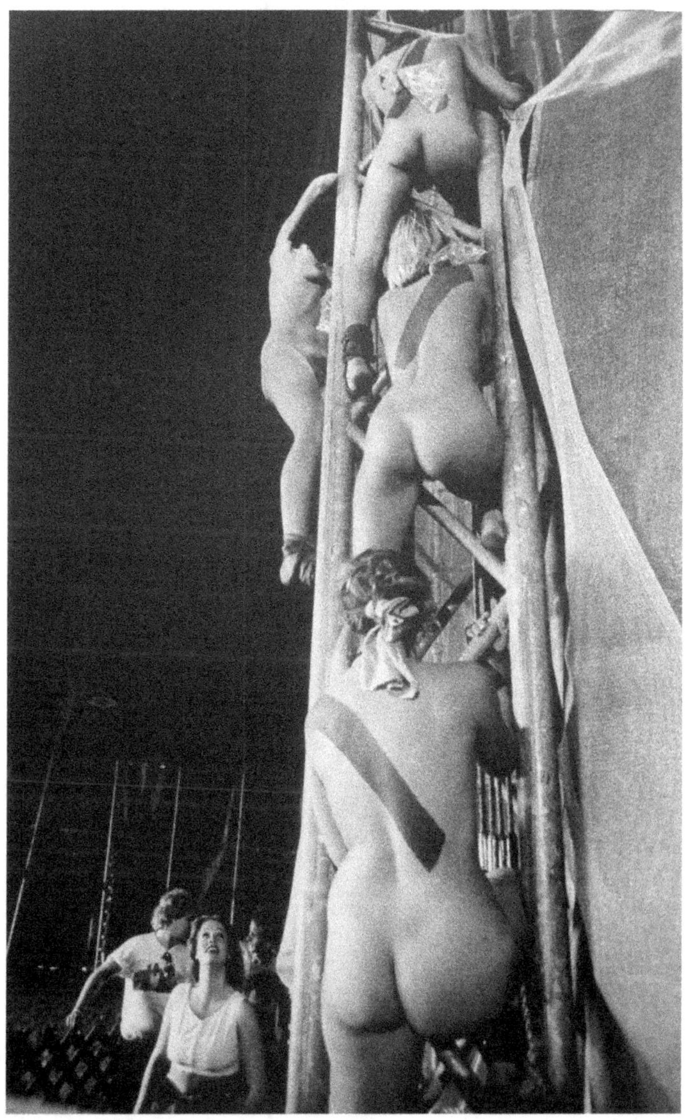

Figure 4.6 Climbing installation "The Tower of Butts"

Source: Photo by Kim Agersten, Polfoto; Jensen 2003:206

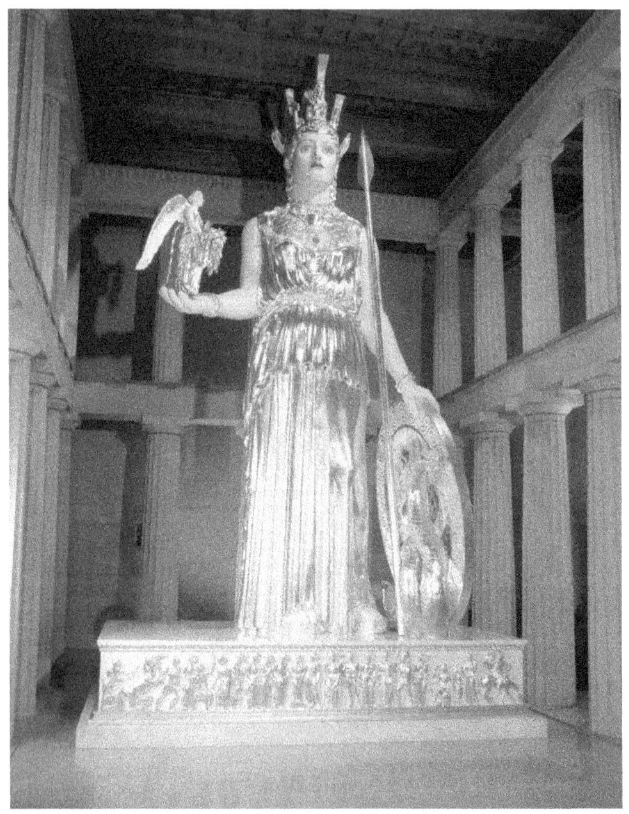

Figure 4.7 Athena, Parthenon, Nashville's Art Museum

Source: Wikimedia

> was organized by the then newly launched festival radio, which was founded by a group of students for the purpose of telling the rest of the Roskilde audience what was going on in their world. . . .
>
> In 2008, more women than men participated for the first time; 16 of the 31 participants were female.
>
> (Michael Jose Gonzalez in the GAFFA 2010 music magazine)

During the 1980s, the nudist look at Roskilde Festival declined, and in the 1990s it was just a shadow of what it had been in the 1970s. The image of a "naturist" Roskilde Festival then increasingly became

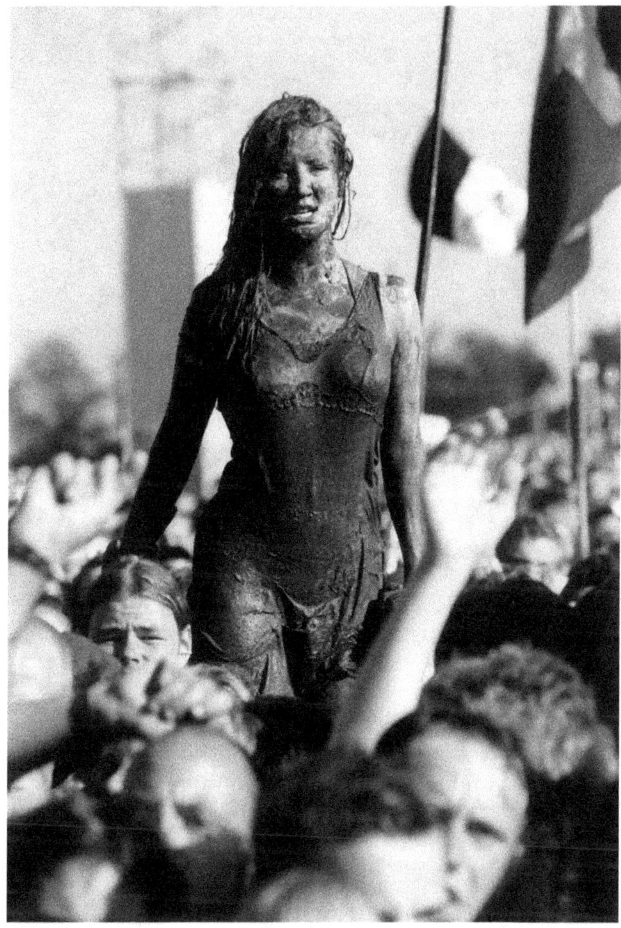

Figure 4.8 A winner of a mud wrestling contest at the 2003 Roskilde Festival

Source: Photo by Kim Agersten, Polfoto; Jensen 2003

a 1970s myth, and newspapers, magazines, and TV gladly spiced up their photo series and reports with archive stills and clips from the 70s. This is when the 25-year-old mythic festival radio established a commemorative marker and transformed the event into ritual. And for past 13 years, it has manifested itself as a "traditional legend" and an intensely media-covered attraction.

The Naked Race is thus both a celebration and a revitalization of the original festival's nudist look.

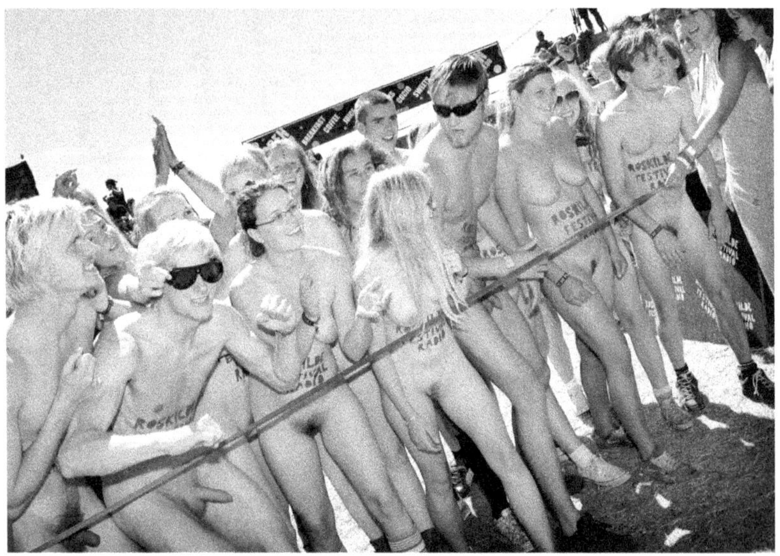

Figure 4.9 Before the start: The Naked Race at the 2009 Roskilde Festival

Source: Photo by Thomas Lekfeldt, Ekstra Bladet, Polfoto

The Naked Race is an ideological-visual brand for the festival, on the same level as mud wrestling and the Orange Stage.

Free sex

Roskilde Festival does not hold any orgies and organized or unorganized orgies do not take place during the festival. The mud wrestling and the Naked Race, supplemented by other changing nude activities, replace the orgies. On the other hand, a free sex life does exist:

> Summer and sun mean only the smallest garments are taken out of backpacks and suitcases at the Roskilde Festival. This is enjoyed by the many single people who walk around the camping area.
>
> One of them is 19-year-old Anne Katrine Jørgensen from Frederiksberg. In a comfortable camping chair and slightly hidden behind a pair of large sunglasses, she tries to make contact with the many lightly-dressed guys who come walking past her camp. . . .

> "I got the most sex in 2006, which was a real sunshine year. In 2007 it didn't go so well. You wear too much clothes when it rains."
>
> (*MetroXpress's* website at the time:www.metroxpress.dk/roskilde-festival/vis-os-bryster-eller-giv-en-l/pTeifD!10_1552-83/)

In the stream of "Best Experience Mails' that the Roskilde Festival received after the 2000 festival, sex and love experiences occupied a very large space. The following examples cover the spectrum quite well:

> *Hooray for the gray igloo*
>
> Very early on a Sunday morning I thought I had partied enough for that day and wanted to go to bed. There was, however, a small problem: We lived in a silver-gray igloo, which was among 100,000 other silver gray igloos!
>
> Overpowered by fatigue, I thought I had found the right igloo, crawled in and slipped into a sleep coma. The next morning, I woke up and there was a strange guy standing there, glowering down at me. He wondered what I was doing in his tent. But he took it nicely, and we plan to get married next summer.
>
> (Erik Jensen 2003:122)

> *Swedish open air sex*
>
> I woke up the next morning to the sound of "oooh, uhhh, uhhh, yes, yes, ohhh!" There were two Swedes lying there screwing under our awning! I decided to give them time to finish and walked quietly out for coffee and breakfast. When I got back, they were still going at it, so I told them, "Okay, folks, now it's time to go!" But the girl, who was on top at the time just looked at me and said, "It's ok, just eat on." I turned to my companion and asked what he thought about this. He just replied, "Me and my girlfriend have been watching for an hour; it's the best porn movie we've ever seen."
>
> (Erik Jensen 2003:125)

Using the concept of performance analysis, we can thus determine that an eight-day stay at a Roskilde Festival puts one in a liminal state of lost impulse control. We have already seen how the authorities handle the intake of cannabis, euphoric substances and alcohol. But as far as sex and nudity are concerned, there is no such authority or boundaries at all as long as it is a matter of mutual consent.

In Victor Turner's liminality system, unlimited sexuality becomes both the effect of and the symbol of freedom and loss of inhibitions:

Breach: Freedom is awakened or advertised
Crisis: Freedom unfolds, unrestricted and unlimited
Redressive Process: Freedom is channeled, amplified, or repeated
Reintegration: Freedom ends or temporarily stabilized or in a permanent relationship

For many festival participants, the ten festival days thereby become a kind of liminal "kick" or "hit," which must be repeated indefinitely or until the "right one" is found.

#MeToo

In 2017, with the rape and sexual violation #MeToo debate at full tilt, there were twelve inquiries into sexual assaults at the festival. Five of the women survivors were interviewed for the Danish newspaper *Politiken*'s series "Roskilde Without Consent" (25 June–2 July 2017), which dealt directly with the character of the rapes, the brutality of the rapists, the police's lack of respect for the victims and the arbitrariness of the judicial system. This series drew a portrait of the dark side or subculture of unrestricted sexuality. Incidents of sexual assault and rape have always taken place during the festival, but to an extent that crept under the radar regarding both the objective recording of these incidents and their psychological after effects. These sexual violations have always been an undesirable part of the "free sex" subculture, but never to the extent where it might undermine Turner's liminality scheme or the prevailing sense of communitas.

In 2018, the festival launched a strategy against sexual assault, a collaboration with rape medical treatments, women's centers, the police, and judicial authorities. The Dionysian subculture, if it continues to grow – in reality or in the media – could become the bacterium that kills the festival. Therefore, these violations must be controlled by all means necessary, but at the same time the exercise of free and unrestrained voluntary sexuality needs to be ensured. This is the festival's greatest future dialectical challenge.

The accident

During a concert, the ultimate liminal state for a festival participant is to be found in the "mosh pit," immediately below the stage. Here one actively or passively can seek out the physical press of bodies above and all around, or give/receive blows and kicks to/from the wild dancers. Immediately after, the post-liminal phase is characterized by "bruises, twisted ankles, broken bones and worse" (Reinholdt Nielsen 2003:258).

On 30 June 2000, at 11 o'clock in the evening a hundred or so of the 50,000–60,000 festival participants in the open area in front of the Orange Stage found themselves in this liminal field. In the mosh pit below the stage where Pearl Jam had been playing for half an hour, people began to fall down because of the many crowd surfers. They toppled onto and into each other and were crushed beneath those who pressed down from above. The security guards tried to stop the music and free the ones who had fallen, but nearly 20 minutes passed before the guards were able to convince the public that this was indeed a calamity – and then pulled nine lifeless figures out of the mosh pit (see Figure 4.10).

Neither the festival management, the police, the press nor the public prosecutor wanted to or was able to place the blame. On their arrival at the Orange Stage, the police believed that Pearl Jam, as performing band, must clearly be the direct cause of the accident, but after violent protests from the band, the police allowed that the festival management and the orchestra were equally responsible. This was not accepted by Pearl Jam, however, who wanted the blame placed entirely on the festival management. The police then diplomatically chose to conclude that the accident was due to "a coincidence of circumstances . . . where the public's behavior was the most essential" (Jensen 2003:83), which was also confirmed by subsequent investigations.

The reality is that the culprit had a divine character and is called Dionysus. He has had great experience and has produced similar accidents over several millennia. His specialty is ritual behavior of the audience in the performative space, a liminal universe of alcohol, drugs, dance, and eroticism, and the Roskilde Festival's famous brand for 30 years offered precisely this performative space:

> For a festival like Roskilde, which is one of the largest and wildest in Northern Europe, it's always been about going after the rush

> with its quick hit of freedom and irresponsibility. Accompanied by rock music that has never attended the school of fine manners or sent its small, knobby-kneed offspring to eager-to-please kindergartens.
>
> The music encouraged dance rituals and patterns that organizers needed to adhere to while ensuring everyone's safety without disturbing or destroying the experience. This experience, that has a Dionysian character, is named after the Greek god of joy and partying. But Dionysus was not just the god of joy. The Greeks also called him "the human culprit."
>
> (Jensen 2003:80–81)

The rock festival is the type of festival where ritual must be fully integrated into the concert performance, which is seen as the audience and bands' actual "gathering" place.

The festival participants seek authenticity – and through this meet the unpredictable, the interesting, the complex, and the insistent. This is how the liminal space is established that the festival participants, for some hours, can enter into centered on the temporary "transportation" that takes place during the concert. "In this phase, the participants (i.e. the audience) will be free from the demands of the outside world and feel at ease and a sense of community. The feeling that Richard Schechner calls "communitas" takes on both an official and a spontaneous manifestation" (Harsløf 2011:203).

But, unlike theater, film, dance, and performance presentations, the rock festival always has a porous backstop no matter how much one tries to secure it, it will always be tested.

The Dionysian quest for authenticity and liminality will always be there. The performative space is not known for surveillance and safety equipment. Dionysus will always be at Roskilde.

The festival's leader

Roskilde Festival's leader Leif Skov helped carry some of the deceased young people back over the fence on the night of the accident. During the following two years, he was the central figure regarding both the police investigations and the extensive security changes. Leif Skov met and spoke to the grieving parents from Denmark, Sweden, Europe, and Australia, mostly for atonement and support, but also to deal with the legal charges and claims. In the absence of police and prosecution's assignation of a legally guilty party parts of the press chose to judge for themselves. Most notably the Danish newspaper

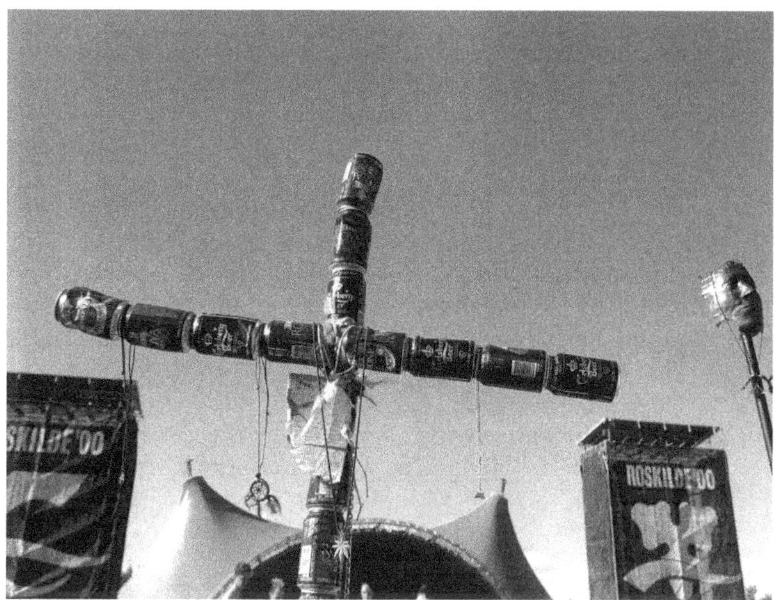

Figure 4.10 A cross made of empty beer cans was spontaneously erected in front of the Orange Stage for the nine young men who lost their lives at the festival

Source: Polfoto; Jensen 2003:86

Politiken, whose editor in chief wrote in December 2000, "It was the Roskilde Festival's responsibility that nine young men were suffocated." In another op-ed piece in February 2001: "Politiken called for the festival manager's resignation" (Journalisten.dk, 27 June 2001). The Danish newspaper *Information*, on 5 July 2000, under the headline "Leif the Top-Down Leader," published a critical portrait based solely on anonymous sources:

> The head of the Roskilde Festival, Leif Skov, is both a grassroots and top notch citizen. He is talented and uncompromising, but also conceited and willful – and not accustomed to harsh criticism. . . . He was initially characterized as competent and unique and of great importance for Danish music and cultural life. But with that said, he is also controlling, conceited and arrogant. . . .

> Leif Skov has maintained his street credibility by cultivating his image as a *plenum*-democratic grass-rooter with preference for not quite young rock music. . . . Yet – or perhaps for this reason – he is held in high esteem and honored by the provincial town's best citizens. In 1998 he became ambassador for Roskilde city and in 1999 became a Knight of Dannebrog [the Danish flag].
>
> (Kim Larsen, Information 5 July 2000)

The 2001 festival, however, was planned meticulously, from the music program (see p. 115) to the memorial with nine birch trees, nine memorial stones, and a center stone with the inscription "How fragile we are." As Leif Skov tells it:

> I gave the hardest speech of my life at the ceremony, which I changed at least 100 times before delivering. For thousands, the opening, with its words and music, was a great release. Also the unveiling of the memorial site. Many regained their strength and peace.
>
> (Jensen 2003:201)

The difficulty with the speech was its disposition. While Pericles in 431/30 BCE, with his postulate on the necessity of war (and thus of human loss), could afford to embark on the excellence of society and the state, and ultimately encourage rather than condone the survivors, Leif Skov had to start with regret. However, this had to be fixed in its genre so that it did not acquire legal validity. Leif Skov chose poetry and espoused on the theme of the memorial stone and on the fragility of human life:

> It's been a long, dreary year and many moons since last summer, when some 70,000 people came to Roskilde seeking excitement and togetherness. You and we knew and still know that life is fragile, not least when we use it searching for dreams and drive. Nine young people lost their lives at Roskilde Festival last summer. They too came here for the excitement. Music and festivals must never cause pain or death.
>
> (Skov 2001:34)

Then Leif Skov remembered those who died by name and sent his and the festival's thoughts to the relatives. The festival owes them in the future, he points out, searching out all potential risks and eliminating or minimizing them. This is the festival's duty and responsibility. But the festival participants also had duties: "However – with almost 100,000 people on this site – we need your understanding, cooperation – and your care" (Skov 2001:34). Finally, he thanked for the warm support and for the suggestions that poured into the festival's organizers and volunteers in the form of letters and emails over the past year.

With this, Leif Skov, in his dramaturgy, arrived at the Pericles "point of no return." Now it was about the festival's survival as an institution, and the city-state event in dialogue with Denmark and world society:

> Roskilde Festival is not a main thing in itself – and has never been. You should rather see Roskilde as part of a culture that wants to present music and make room for dialogue, understanding, excitement and good experiences. In the light of last year's tragedy and in respect of the lives who were so meaninglessly lost, we will ask you – along with us – to protect the idea of the interaction between free spirits and the music culture by sending the message to politicians, authorities, parents, and others that it is possible AND important to get together and keep up dialogue and develop understanding."
>
> (Skov 2001:34)

Then the reading of the Danish poet Morten Søndergaard's poem "Site Seeing Zoom" followed, where two of the verses read:

> I was put up against a whitewashed wall
> blindfolded and knew
> I was going to die.
>
> But I did not die,
> just fell out of time
> and that which was my life
> was marching by
> continuing into a soft darkness
> where all the doors are ajar.
>
> (Skov 2001:35)

Then the composer and jazz trumpeter Palle Mikkelborg and his orchestra played "Eternity's Sunrise." Leif Skov completed the ceremony by first asking the festival participants to turn to the west "where the sun is going down" (and where the memorial grove was established). Then he reassured the survivors that they have his and the festival's deepest respect and love.

Leif Skov's artistic feat was what one could call his performance of a "double Pericles." He took his point of departure in the memorial stone's poetry: "how fragile we are," then reinforced it with Morten Søndergaard's poem and Mikkelborg's music. Although at the same time, he embedded assurances of safety, his demand for collective responsibility, and his direct reference to Danish politicians, authorities, and parents. The message was so crystal clear that it could be formulated poetically.

Leif Skov's performance was an unconditional success and fulfilled all the demands of performance theory, formulated in the past and in the present.

5 Dionysus at Roskilde

Roskilde

The festivals arose from the protests and hippie movements of the '60s in a paradigmatic political and economic climate. The Isle of Wight Festival and Woodstock are transformed into Europe and Roskilde. In Roskilde, the festival myth consolidates into a well-functioning apparatus and a flexible city-state structure – so strong that it can both overcome crises and survive politically. The social and cultural Roskilde Foundation is governed by the city, with its highest official as chairman, thereby ensuring both political legitimacy and an economic foundation. The Roskilde Foundation hires the festival's full-time employees or places municipal employees in the festival management. In its organizational structure, the festival adopts or establishes satellite companies and organizations, as well as finalizes agreements with institutions, cultural and artistic companies, and institutes of higher education. The festival itself can also initiate the construction and operation of new institutions.

Already in 1995, Leif Skov noted in his anniversary article:

> Respect for Roskilde Festival's work and organization has meant that others want to profile themselves via the festival and seek the benefit of the festival's know-how. Copenhagen as a Culture City in 1996 and Roskilde City's 1000 year anniversary in 1998 are examples of this. Representatives of the Roskilde Festival had a central position in work committees connected to these events.
>
> (Rung 1995:14)

After 2000, the festival participated in the building of a new innovative city "Musicon" located between the festival area and Roskilde's town center and the festival was responsible for establishing a folk high school there as well. Here, the festival would play the central role both in the new city (regarding innovations and tourism), in Roskilde city (regarding education and commerce) and in the future, to an even greater extent than now, it would integrate Roskilde University into its activities, development plans and experience-economic research.

The festival has survived the changing political (democratic) systems of welfare social-democracy to state liberalism, and it is important that it is never associated with political parties or systems. On the other hand, the municipal "city-state anchoring" is vital.

The only thing that could put an end to the Roskilde Festival would be a new (politically and ideologically supported) state religion. Christianity was opposed to nudity and extreme culture (sports competitions and Dionysian festivals), as was Protestantism for a long time, and Catholicism and Islam still are. The Roskilde Festival must therefore maintain and develop an anarcho-democratic ritual paradigm that can reject and resist actions or attacks from all existing or emerging religious or populist parties at any time. These actions or attacks constitute the real danger to the festival's existence.

The Roskilde Festival is an enterprise of great importance for the art and cultural economic landscape. The Athenian state ran a festival, managed by a designated official (archon), who selected and employed artists, and tendered productions and operations. To ensure the Dionysian festival's continued existence, popularity, and growth, the state built new attractions around the theater: a concert hall, a sports facility and a hospital/health center. During the same period, the city-state symbol, the Parthenon Temple was completed, decorated with the city-state's myths, history and festival scenes.

In 1972, Roskilde City's senior official, who was the chairman of the Roskilde Foundation, appointed the municipal employee (the leader of the Youth Club), who was to join the festival management. The Roskilde Foundation employed management and staff for the festival secretariat. Today, an employee of the festival management selects and hires artists. Today, festival management, though still responsible to the Roskilde Group, handles production and operational tasks and potential licenses. Roskilde's various associations have the opportunity to run a large number of food and beverage venues. As mentioned (on p. 126), the lack of effective countering of sex abuse in the new #MeToo media space could also become a serious threat.

The code of Roskilde

As we saw previously (p. 79), the Dionysus Feast was an integral part of a cultural and societal code that I choose to call "The Code of

Dionysus." It developed within a paradigmatic time period as a transformation from a theoretical and aesthetic performative space into a number of concrete practices.

A similar code for a transformation of the Roskilde Festival's performative space, "The Code of Roskilde," can be developed within the time paradigm of 1945 until today.

The postwar years were strongly influenced by a restrictive moral code and communication structure. Thus, in the years leading up to the 1960s, religious based sexual moral rules (prohibition of abortion) and upbringing practices (corporal punishment) were still in place. At the same time, the performative space of the period was filled with new genres and expressions – in philosophy, music, dance, literature, theater, visual arts, and athletics/sports.

Europe underwent a major change during this period. The developed fascist governments (Italy and Germany) became part of the Western European collective consciousness, flanked by Eastern bloc communism and Spanish, Portuguese, and Greek Falangism. The Western European concept of liberty was greatly expanded – much influenced by similar philosophical ideas and expressions in the United States (especially the philosopher Herbert Marcuse). This not only resulted in a number of concrete freedoms, but these western European "freedoms" became such a strong symbol for eastern European populations that it led to uprisings and also to the fall of Southern European dictatorships. In the years after 1968, a new powerful collective European awareness emerged, so powerful that it could connect Northern and Central Europe with the new Southern European democracies and growing dissident groups in the Eastern bloc countries.

These new freedoms, which resulted in a liberalized way of life and communication structures – all at once allowed for and created new forms of experience and ways of being together. And here, festivals were the most visible, both in size and in practice. Events with such content and vast scope had not been seen since antiquity.

A number of humanistic, philosophical, Eastern or neo-religious values freely and unmistakably became part of the thinking, debate, and practice of western life. And from the end of the 1960s, it all came together, greatly helped by the new media, into a number of more firmly ritualized practices – most obviously fairs (books, art, furniture, food), festival weeks, carnivals, festivals, as well as athletic competitions and matches in the increasing number of parks, sports arenas (see Figure 5.1).

The code of Roskilde

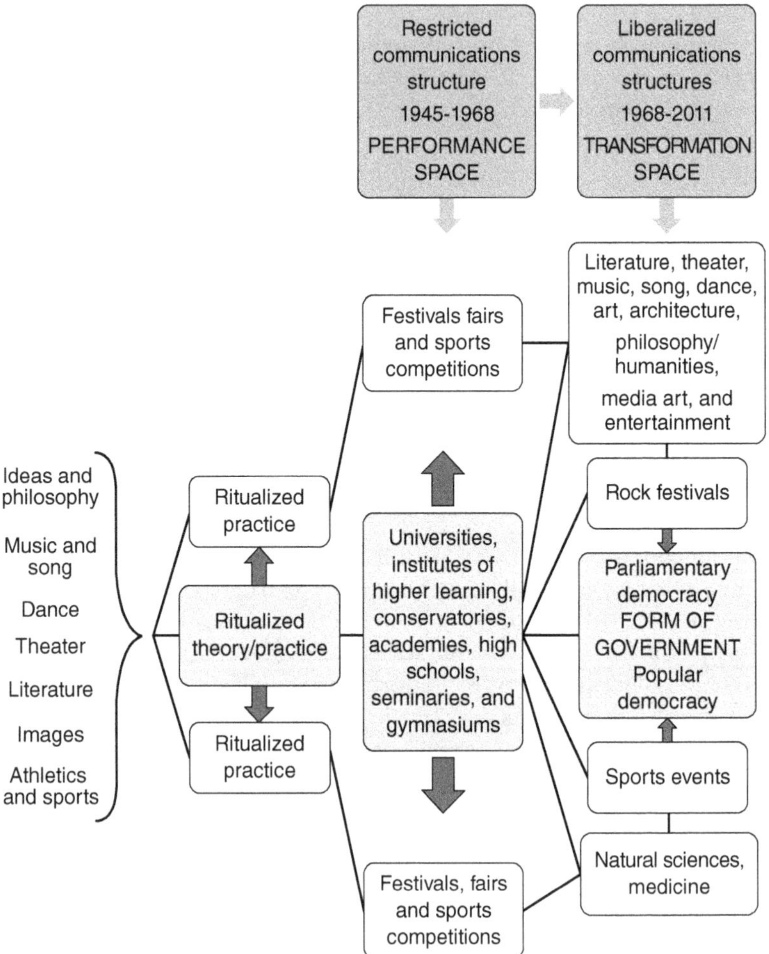

Figure 5.1 Communications model for the rock festival's performance space

However, at the same time, a combination of ritualized theory and practice emerged. New university centers, art schools, educational institutes and gymnasiums attracted the massive generation of baby boomers away from agriculture, industry, crafts and service to extensive pedagogic, artistic, media or academic educations, bringing with it the accompanying social status, new lifestyles and influence on the collective consciousness.

Starting in the late 1960s, concept-based knowledge was expanded and the number of university faculties increased – first and foremost, the social sciences faculty. In addition, a number of new subjects and disciplines emerged culminating around the turn of the millennium with preventive health science, humanistic technology, as well as information, design, performance and cultural sciences.

The great expansion of knowledge that took place in European societies during the 1960s also led to the splitting of individual nations' collective consciousness into the logically innovative and the irrationally narrative-based consciousness and understanding of the world. The latter resulted politically in the emergence of populist parties, which, although differing in terms of ideological form, share the denial of scientific knowledge as a common foundation.

The two dominant political and philosophical positions in the performative space since 1970 have also been knowledge and pushing boundaries on the one hand, and knowledge-denying and border-preserving on the other. In countries where the populist position periodically has had parliamentary influence on political power (for example, Italy, Austria, Holland, Poland, the Czech Republic, Slovakia, Hungary, Norway, and Denmark) the concept of education and science has undergone a complete change: the populist scientific narrative, human and social sciences are either ideologically/strategically required research or for dissemination and entertainment – as opposed to medicine and the natural sciences, which manifest themselves in hospitals, laboratories and research institutions to promote human healing, improve transportation opportunities and make new "discoveries" in space.

As a result of this understanding of science, medicine and the natural sciences are subject to the rules of sport. Both the declared rules, about fairness and the undeclared rules, about abuse and unethical behavior.

After 1968, philosophy and the humanities are thus separated in the "freedom paradigm" from the natural sciences and medicine, which are now categorized with sport, while the social sciences along with art become part of an entertainment and media-borne universe. The new disciplinary order and logic of postmodernism evolved into information technology and functions as interactive social media. TV is reduced to an entertainment media (also in terms of the news), just as DVDs and CDs lose value and importance in terms of live concerts and live performances (reduced to documentation and advertising) due to downloading and file sharing. The combination of new freedoms and new technologies' continual transformation of thought, consciousness, conditions, cohabitation, and socially related functions enables development and changes of rules and logic as we consistently see in technology management and sport, where the game and the rules keep changing. However, they still keep moving toward the increasingly simple, clear, and understandable – always with the aim of gaining insight, happiness, victory, fame, and self-forgetfulness.

It is in this ritual configuration that parliamentary democracy's thinking and practiced social life develops alternatives. Throughout the major confrontational power structure (NATO-Warsaw Pacts) that concluded with the fall of the Berlin wall in 1989, the rising power of oil states, economic growth in Japan and China, during simultaneous censorship and liberalization, two different forms of popular protest appeared in Western democracies: an anarcho-liberal faction, with socialist segments expressed through the '68 movement, and a populist, anti-bureaucratic faction, expressed through newly formed political parties rejecting both the values and lifestyle of the '68ers as well as classical bourgeois education. While toward the end of the century the populist parties found their suitable and well-functioning platform in the TV-mediated image of democracy, the anarcho-liberal group established the "great festival" as its dominant platform – with the Roskilde Festival as the largest in Northern Europe.

Along with sports competitions and TV-mediated entertainment, rock festivals have established themselves as the highest form of integrated ritual and entertainment. This is translated into, but never separated from, the totality of a system of social and political rules of behavior that safeguard against individual extinction and collective destruction. However, the festival has its own authenticity, expressed in actions that both protect and secure the individual's unrestricted freedom and private rights. It is, as previously shown, at the rock festival that one can live out the rush, challenge oneself and exhibit one's sexual life in the performative space – and in extreme cases as an ultimate necessity – stage one's own death.

The rock festival is today the performative space that can contain all rituals and all entertainment (all genres), translated into rules, games, and play, for all social and political entities. The festivals are substantiated in terms of content by rock, blues, and folk music. The music is the genesis for both the festival's presentation forms and alternative thought-structures for participant behavior. The festival is "a living anarcho-liberal democracy," as well as a knowledge system that incorporates modern sciences such as design, visual art, performance, environmental technology, informatics, acoustics, and architecture.

Both populism and anarcho-liberalism, with their two large activity and media platforms, have had a decisive influence on the change of performative space over the last twenty years. But where populism has been a major challenge and a strong restructuring factor for classical education, the festival has increasingly taken on the mantle as a marker for freedom, retention of human rights and individual values.

One might say, with a slight rewriting of J.R. Green (Green 1994:12), that the festival as musical performance and lived authenticity is closely linked to the basic idea of democracy and thereby stimulates this, just as democracy itself, for more than 100 years, in the formulation of still new freedoms (voting rights for women, the abolition of censorship, the abolition of corporal punishment, abortion rights), created the possibility for the festival's existence.

Also, Richard Schechner's previously cited (p. 79–80) three purposes of festival performance are clearly valid for the rock festival's performance:

- To maintain friendly relations.
- To exchange goods, mates, trophies, techniques.
- To show and exchanges dances, songs, stories.

Furthermore, I think these performances followed rhythms familiar to us in:

- Gathering.
- Playing out an action or actions.
- Dispersing.

(Schechner 1988:175–176)

As we also saw with the analysis of the Dionysus Festival, it is in the "Dispersing" phase where recognition and thus social regeneration takes place. "The Code of Dionysus" herewith gets its counterpart in "The Code of Roskilde": The Roskilde Festival, like the Dionysus Festival, has the stated purpose of wanting to change humanity. The classical performances (theater, dance, music), like rock festivals "portray efficacious ritual practice, which become in a sense rituals within a ritual." Also like classical performances, the festival can be described as "*efficacious myths*, shaping the way the Athenian audience understood rituals which are performed outside the Dionysia" (Wiles 2000:37), that is to say, the way festival participants understand rituals which are performed outside the Roskilde Festival.

"The Code of Roskilde" is one such "efficacious myth" – arising from and formed by free thinking and corporal expressions, images, music and song, dance and narratives – and then ritualized in theory and practice in a performative space, transformed and constituted into the institution of the Roskilde Festival.

6 The great festival

The performative space

In my documentation, descriptions, and analyses of the Dionysus Festival and the Roskilde Festival, I have occasionally exemplified and illustrated with references from antiquity's festival conditions relating to the present day, or compared classical ideas and actions with modern ideas and actions, just as I, in my introduction, compiled two descriptions of festival accidents, one in 458 BCE and one in 2000 CE.

This does not mean that I believe in historical parallels or suggest that "history repeats itself." On the other hand, I am interested in historical structures that have been cleansed of the ideology, religion, morality, politics, pedagogy, and interpretation of recent times and can be compared to "pure" expressions of human aspiration and development in a given performative space.

For the participant, a feast or festival is first and foremost "lived content." For organizers, producers and "owners," it's just as much about practiced economy, organization, logistics, politics, prestige and not least, honor. The aim of the festival and the festival organizers is to create a historical paradigm – and personally to get their monument preserved in marble, introduced into the history books or expressed in the media. The same goes for the performing artists. These four stakeholders – festival participants, organizers, artists and entrepreneurs etc. – form two crucial groups, the first and the last of which together form a large and significant part of the population: Festival participants and suppliers of all the physical necessities, through their involvement as both "users" or "sellers," enjoy indisputable aesthetic, social and economic benefits. On the other hand, organizers and artists reap the power, the credit and (for the latter) the great financial gain. Finally, the host city-state (or the entire host country) is rewarded with increased revenue, taxes and VAT, as well as launching a number of secondary activities (new businesses, state funding of infrastructure, foundation financing of new institutions), and also the pleasure and satisfaction for citizens and voters – a good will that can be translated into political decisions and innovation.

The festival management estimates the Roskilde Festival's annual turnover at 450 million Danish crowns, with a participation of 100,000 people (80,000 full time and 20,000 one-day tickets, plus 40,000 volunteers, media people, musicians, sound people and suppliers). In addition, there is extra revenue for the city of Roskilde of 200–300 million Danish crowns (Danielsen tells me in a note 6 November 2011). If we assume that between 15,000–20,000 participated in the Dionysus Festivals in the 5th and 4th centuries BCE, the city-state of Athens may have had an annual revenue, converted into today's purchasing power, of 50–75 million Danish crowns. Alone, the sheer size and significance of this amount for the city of Athens can explain why the Dionysus Festival continued unhindered for a variety of occupying powers and their tax collectors.

Most importantly, however, it must be stated that the Dionysus Festival was administered and produced based on a carefully tested and consistently developed concept. In addition to the extensive performance program of song, music, theater, readings and sports with their associated economic, production and development plans, as well as requisitions and the organization of stage management, the concept contained plans for information, communications, logistics, boarding, catering, lodging, hygiene and jurisdiction.

Based on the specific knowledge we have about the Dionysian Festival's anchorage in the urban city-state, plus its organization, scope and concept, I find it permissible to compare this to the Roskilde Festival's corresponding conditions.

Here similarities and differences between Dionysian Festivals and the Roskilde Festivals can be seen. The similarities are striking.

The Dionysus Festivals 500s BCE through 300s BCE	The Roskilde Festivals since 1970
Festival organizer: City-state of Athens	*Festival organizer:* The Roskilde Festival Association
Festival management: Each year, the state's political leadership appoints an official to plan and lead the festival	*Festival management:* The association's board (which also represents the municipality) is included in the festival management and hires one (or two) responsible festival coordinator(s)/director(s)
State and municipality: The state and the municipalities *do not* contribute financially to the festival. The state alone takes care of the practical management. The festival's feast (roast beef and wine) *can* however be paid by the city-state.	*State and municipality:* The state and the municipality of Roskilde *do not* contribute financially to the festival. The Roskilde Festival has a close and mutually binding practical collaboration with Roskilde Municipality. However, the municipality *can* provide representative dinners at the festival's restaurants
Sponsors: The festival leader appoints sponsors among the many who have signed up. The criteria are financial solidity and documented project management skills, since the sponsors are also producers of the activity they finance	*Sponsors:* The Board and the director (today the Board) select sponsors from those who regularly sign up. The criteria are ethical and product-oriented (secondary benefits such as beer)
Artists: The festival leader appoints the writers who may participate in the year's tragedy and comedy competition	*Artists:* The music director will book participating international and well-known national bands. Other national bands are selected after submitted applications with demo- attachments
Symbolism: Pericles initiates and persuades the Popular Assembly to let the Parthenon Temple be erected and decorated as a symbol of the city-state's strength and wealth	*Symbolism:* Festival Director Leif Skov initiates and persuades the Association to purchase, renovate and set up The Orange Canopy (The Rolling Stones' original tour stage setting) as a symbol of the festival's status and strength

Figure 6.1 The Dionysian Festival and the Roskilde Festival: Differences and Similarities.

Festival area and locations: Athens Hostels, private accommodations The Agora (The Marketplace) Theater, concert hall, sports area The Acropolis The Parthenon	*Festival area and locations:* Roskilde Campgrounds area The festival venue The stages The Media City Backstage
Festival venue: A scaffolding owner receives the concession of setting up spectator seating and the backstage wall and collecting the entrance fee (his payment for erection and use).	*Festival venue:* Structures and renovations are managed by the festival's architect. Pavilions, tents, stages, lights/sound, installations etc. are designated for a number of suppliers
Duration: The festival lasts 8 days. 3 + 4 + 1 days: 1: presentation, 2: procession and concluding festival banquet, 3: choir competition, 4: comedy competition, 5–7: tragedy and satyr play competition, 8: evaluation	*Duration:* The festival lasts 8/10 days. 4 + 4 days, today 5 + 4 + 1 days: 4 days in the camp area, 4 concert days: today 5 days in the camp area, 4 concert days and 1 day of departure
Presentation: On the first day the participating authors and sponsors/producers (choregi) present their cast of actors, choir members and musicians for the public	*Presentation:* The festival management organizes various events for journalists, reviewers and professionals in the Media City
Ceremonies: The image/sculpture of the god Dionysus is carried in an evening torch lit procession from a shrine outside the city through the city gate to the Athens marketplace, and from there, the following morning to the Dionysus Temple where sacrificial animals are slaughtered. The same evening and night, there is wild partying and dancing through the streets.	*Ceremonies:* The Orange Stage canopy is erected. The fence is toppled in connection with the opening to the festival area (though only in the years 2007–2010). The Naked Race on Saturday afternoon (after 1998)

Figure 6.1 Continued

Artistic program: 10 dithyrambic boy choirs (song/dance) and 10 dithyrambic male choirs, three tetralogies (1 tetralogy = 3 tragedies and 1 satyr play), 5 comedies, and poetry reading	*Artistic program:* Rock music and related genres on seven (today six) stages played by internationally known and Danish bands. In addition, specially invited ensembles from other genres (for example, opera)
Music performance: Monodies in various scales and rhythms for choral singing and choral dancing, performed on stage as rhythmic and corporal performances	*Music performance:* Rock in major/minor scales, 4/4 beat, performed on stage as rhythmic and corporal performances
Instruments: Aulos or double aulos (auloi) in several variations (soprano, alto, tenor, baritone) with very powerful and intense sound and with great potential emotional impact	*Instruments:* Guitar, keyboard, bass, drums (possibly wind and percussion instruments) and singing voices with very powerful electric amplification and with great potential emotional impact
Judges: The judging panel consists of a representative from each of the city-state's 10 fyles (districts) – and the audience	*Judges:* Daily newspapers (Danish and foreign), rock reporters - and the audience
Contests: Competitions on the actual festival stage for – choir/dance, tetralogy, best tetralogy poet, best actor, best aulos player (oboist/shawm blower), best sponsor/producer. Away from the festival stage are poetry readings and various sports competitions (wrestling, running, spear throwing, discus, shot-putting)	*Contests:* Many competitions are held in the camping area, all of them non-artistic. In the festival area (since 1998), on the penultimate afternoon the Naked Race is held, where the fastest man and woman win a ticket for the next year's festival. In addition, knowledge competitions (for example, who knows most about the festival)
Volunteers: The 1000 amateurs in the boys and men's singing/dancing choirs participate voluntarily as representatives of their district in the competition for best choirs, in two categories. 500 boys and 500 men	*Volunteers:* Approximately 30,000 volunteers resolve a large number of practical tasks and at the same time have free access to the festival and certain facilities. Many work much more than the 24 hours set as a minimum

Figure 6.1 Continued

Ticket price: Entrance fee per day. The entrance fee is paid to the scaffolding owner but this stopped in 330s BCE when the city state built stone seating as a replacement for the scaffold owners' wooden grandstands.	*Ticket price:* One entry fee for the entire festival. In recent years, daily entrance fees were approximately half of the fee amount for the entire festival
Guests: Politicians, strategists (war councils), ecclesiastical authorities, foreign ministers and partners (allies), as well as representatives of conquered countries	*Guests:* Roskilde Municipality's politicians and officials are invited to the festival, as is Roskilde parish's bishop. The same applies to ministers, parliamentary politicians and ministerial officials, as well as regional politicians.
Dionysian culture: Wine, dance, nude culture and euphoric drinking	*Dionysian culture:* Beer, liquor, cannabis, dance, nude culture and euphoric substances
Illegal subculture: Occurrence of rape during the festival. Literary example, and therefore only of fictional value, about rape of slave women by free citizens (men). No sources indicate sanctions	*Illegal subculture:* Rape during the festival is publicized and reported with high media focus after the #MeToo disclosures in 2017. Resolution on strategy for elimination, support for victims and stricter sanctions
Generosity: Prison detainees were released during the festival and overdue debts could not be collected	*Generosity:* Free admission for age 50+ participants at the festival's last day (in recent years 60+)
Evaluation: On the festival's last day, everyone interested in Dionysian theater gathers with an opportunity to give criticism or praise. Unacceptable conditions are assessed and possibly, guilty persons are fined or punished	*Evaluation:* All work groups prepare a post-festival critique and at a weekend meeting in September, the management's conclusions are discussed, as well as incoming proposals from the 32 area managers.
Regional political constellation: The Delian League vs. the Peloponnese Confederation	*Global political constellation:* NATO vs. the Warsaw Pact (until 1989). Then various east-west confrontation constellations

Figure 6.1 Continued

As can be seen from the table above, both festivals were initiated by the "city-state." The Dionysian Feast came about as populist outreach in connection with the overthrow of the Solonic democracy in approximately 560 BCE, but with similar justification was maintained by the City Council on the return of democracy again in 510 BCE. The idea for the celebration/festival, however, came from outsiders – in Greece from peasants and craftsmen, in Roskilde from high school students and music organizers/musicians. The festival was taken over by the "city-state" and administered by municipal officials. "The city-state" does not contribute directly to the festival – indirectly, in Athens, with free access to festival areas. Representative facilities were available at the Acropolis with the city-state's center for architecture, art, and design, as well as the Parthenon Temple. The opening night festival dinner for all participants was probably paid for by the "city-state." In Roskilde, the livestock fairgrounds is made available for a reasonable rent. Only in the first years did the municipality provide a half-deficit guarantee. Both festivals receive sponsorship support. All participants, except the festival's "volunteers" pay for their own consumption. The municipality can hold representative dinners in the festival's Media City. Especially important media people and guests are invited into the VIP rooms backstage.

In Athens, the festival director designated sponsors among the many manufacturers, contractors, landlords, and traders who want to fund one of the Dionysus Festival's performances. The sponsor is also a producer. At Roskilde, the festival management chooses its sponsors among applicant companies and firms.

In Athens, the festival leader selected creative and performing artists. At Roskilde, the festival management books deals with (economically) accessible and artistically relevant bands, either directly or via booking agencies.

In Athens, the city state chose and financed the festival's symbolism. In the 430s BCE, the head of state, Pericles, initiates and persuades the Popular Assembly to let the Parthenon Temple be erected and embellished as a symbol of the city-state's strength and wealth. At Roskilde, the chairman of the festival director Leif Skov takes the initiative and persuades the Roskilde Festival Association that "The Orange Canopy" should be purchased, restored and set up as a symbol of the festival's status and strength.

Lodging and logistics in Athens consisted of shelters and hostels for private accommodation, the city state's agora, the theater, the concert hall and sports facilities, as well as the Acropolis buildings with the Parthenon Center. At Roskilde, there is a camping area in several sections, a festival site with six or seven stages and the Media City and backstage that is closed for regular festival participants.

In Athens, the owner of the grandstand scaffolding was granted a concession for the setting up of spectator seats and the backstage wall as well as collecting the entrance fee. At Roskilde, the structures and renovation is performed by the festival's architect. Pavilions, tents, stages, lights/sound, installations, etc. are assigned to a number of suppliers, some of which have indirect economic links to the festival. In Athens, the scaffolding owner was paid for a place to sit. At Roskilde, one pays the festival administration a one-time fee for access to the festival area throughout the period.

Both festivals last for eight days. The Dionysus Festival 3 + 4 + 1 days: 1: presentation, 2: procession with concluding festival banquet, 3: choir competition, 4: comedy competition, 5–7: tragedy and satyr play competition, 8: evaluation. The Roskilde Festival 4 + 4 days, today 5 + 4 + 1 days: 4 days in the camp area, 4 concert days, today 5 days in the camp area, 4 concert days and 1 day of departure. Both have fixed ceremonies. In Athens, the image/sculpture of the god Dionysus was taken on the first night of the torch lit procession from a shrine outside the city, carried through the city gate to the city's marketplace and from there, the following morning, brought to the Dionysus Temple, where sacrificial animals were slaughtered. That same evening and night, there was unrestrained partying and dancing through the streets. At Roskilde, the Orange Stage canopy is erected. A small part of the fence around the camping area is toppled as a symbol of opening access to the festival area. Since 1998, a Naked Race on the festival's penultimate afternoon has been a fixed and beloved ceremony.

Both festivals have extensive artistic programs. In Athens, it commenced with ten dithyrambic boy choirs (song/dance) and ten dithyrambic male choirs. Then three tetralogies followed (one tetralogy = three tragedies and one satyr play), five comedies, and poetry readings. Roskilde plays rock music and similar rhythmic genres (world music, folk, jazz, Latin, African) from seven (today six) stages with internationally known and Danish bands. In addition, there are especially invited ensembles from other genres. The musical material, like the instruments and sound systems, was developed for this particular performance form. In Athens, monodies were performed in various scales and a 5/4 beat, but also other rhythms, for choral singing and dancing, staged as rhythmic and corporal performances. At Roskilde, the main genre is rock music, performed in major/

minor scales and a 4/4 beat, also staged as rhythmic and corporal performances. In Athens, the aulos or double aulos (auloi) were used in several variations (soprano, alto, tenor, baritone) with a very powerful and intense sound, with great potential emotional impact. At Roskilde, guitar, keyboard, bass guitar, drums are used, as well as singing voices with very powerful electric amplification, with great potential emotional potential impact.

Judging the performances was completely different in ancient times than the present. In Athens, a panel of judges composed of representatives from each of the ten fyles (districts) was formed. None of these judges was specially trained and they allowed themselves to be swayed by voxpop. At Roskilde, the performances are evaluated by rock critics in daily newspapers. Most of these journalists are permanent and long-standing employees at their respective newspapers and their verdicts are thus of great importance to the bands they are reviewing. However, audience attendance, behavior, and applause also have great influence.

Also regarding the competitions, there is a decisive difference between the ancient and the present day festival. In Athens, the competitions concerned the artistic and sporting disciplines, as well as sponsorship and production skills. On the festival stage itself, there were competitions for best choir/dance, tetralogies, tetralogy writers, actor, aulos player, and sponsor/producer. Away from the festival stage, there were poetry competitions and various sports competitions. Roskilde does not have competitions in the artistic or economic/production areas, and only to some extent for sports. Here, as with a number of quiz competitions, the entertainment is independent or detached from the artistic content. In the camping area many competitions are held, though all of a non-artistic nature. In the festival area, a Naked Race is carried out on the festival's penultimate afternoon (since 1998), where the fastest man and woman win a ticket for the next year's festival. In addition, knowledge competitions are known to take place. The absence of participant-driven competition or the expert artistic assessment is the point at which the present-day festival differs decisively from the ancient festival.

Roskilde Festival has a very special "volunteer culture," which is not known from either antiquity's festivals or for that matter, other modern festivals. Approximately 30,000 volunteers take care of a large number of practical tasks. For 24 hours of work during the festival, they have free entrance and access to certain facilities. Although this "voluntary culture" is not comparable to the 1,000 amateur singers who participated in the Dionysus Festival, it has the same function: to create awareness of the festival and to attract participants among the amateur singers' family and acquaintances.

Both festivals allow and cultivate a rich and uniform goal of Dionysian culture. In Athens, with wine, dance, nude culture and euphoric drinks. At Roskilde with beer, spirits, cannabis, dance, nude culture and euphoric substances. As a consequence, a larger (Athens) or smaller (Roskilde) ambition of generosity is exhibited. In Athens, prison detainees were released during the festival and debts owed could not be collected. In Roskilde, free admission for age 50+ participants is given on the festival's last day (in recent years raised to 60+).

Literary texts indicated the occurrence of rape during the Dionysus Festival in the form of rape of slave women by free citizens (men). No sources tell us anything about sanctions. At the Roskilde Festival, rape is announced and reported during the festival. And now with strong media focus after the #MeToo revelations from large parts of the world in 2017, the festival management has taken the initiative and decided on a strategy for elimination of these incidents, support for the victims, with stricter police and legal sanctions.

Both festivals have a guest policy. In Athens, politicians, strategists, ecclesiastical authorities, foreign ministers and partners were invited, as well as representatives from conquered countries. At Roskilde, Roskilde Municipality's politicians and civil servants are invited, just as Roskilde parish's bishop. The same applies to ministers, parliamentarians and government officials, as well as regional politicians.

Both festivals are finally evaluated. In Athens, on the last day of the festival, everyone interested in Dionysian theater gathered with an opportunity to offer criticism or praise. Objectionable situations were assessed and possibly, guilty persons received fines or penalties. At Roskilde, all work groups prepare a post-festival critique and at a weekend meeting in September, the management's conclusions are discussed, as well as incoming proposals from the 32 area managers.

Both festivals' structure and artistic form grew out of comparable world political situations. In Athens, during the first war (with the Persians), then a cold war and later the city-state war between the two dominant military alliances, the Delian League led by Athens and the Peloponnesian Confederation led by Sparta.

The modern festival developed during the world-wide political bipolar super-power formation of the Cold War and Vietnam War, sustained by two military alliances, NATO and the Warsaw Pact (until 1989). It emerged and found its form parallel to the dismantling of southern European military dictatorships and Falangism (in Greece, Spain, and Portugal), the American Civil Rights Movement and the international struggle against apartheid in South Africa. The creation and formative period of beat and rock music coincides with the construction of the Berlin Wall in 1961 and its fall in 1989.

The Athenian city-state Dionysus Festival, though initiated by a dictatorship, would prove to be a fitting entertainment and performative expression of democracy. The Roskilde Festival also fits in with today's modern democracy. It is the result of a political-administrative initiative in 1971 and still complies with all economic and legal laws and regulations, or adopts special agreements with the authorities wherever desirable and possible. Within this framework, the festival is free to set up themes that don't necessarily correspond to the seated governments or city council majority. In the same way, performing bands can present their texts completely uncensored. In addition, there is the strong media attention to the alternative lifestyle forms and activities to which the festival is subject. The Roskilde Festival can, however, freely set decisive provocative political agendas – as Aristophanes did in 411 BCE with his comedy *Lysistrata* (Women's Rebellion) as a criticism of the war between the Delian League (Athens) and the Peloponnese Confederation (Sparta).

I have demonstrated a structural similarity between the two festivals – through both description and analysis of their historical performative spaces and the resulting "codes." I also believe I have made possible larger structural and some concrete comparisons, evident from the table on pages 142–146.

The many similarities are striking. But perhaps most interesting are the crucial differences, of which performance assessment and the competitions are the most important:

In Athens, performance evaluation was entrusted to festival participants who represented the city-state's ten fyles (districts). These judges were guided by mood, applause and, of course, their own impressions. Although this form of assessment has often been described as arbitrary, one cannot say anything other than that it is audience inclusive, in the sense that it gives the audience ownership of the concerts and performances, and thus to current and relevant tones, rhythms, dances, myths, satirized social and political discourses, and erotic/pornographic god and human universes.

The participants were and remain an interactive audience through all the festival's components – from the possibility of participating in the dithyrambic choirs to voting for artistic winners.

At the Roskilde Festival, interaction takes place on the campground and in the festival area, and most intensely in front of the stages, where some participants are close to the performing artists. There is no doubt that the participants rate the bands and singers with their behavior and applause, but they do not select a winner or a number of winners in different disciplines. The assessments are left to professional media journalists, who hereby gain an irresistible communicative ownership of the festival where they can unimpededly comment on all areas. Of course, media workers are responsible for the functioning of modern democracy, but they might well be complemented by participant panels of judges, texting polls, or similar social and digital forms of expression – institutionalized in an independent headquarters in the Media City. In this way, a two-dimensional form of competition might be established that could insert a competitive element in relation to the performing artists as well as the professional reviewers. Through this, the individual festival participant might develop a stronger ownership bond with the festival.

Ownership of the festival was – and will always be – the guarantee of its authenticity, its fascination, and its continuation as "restored behavior."

Bibliography

Anderson, Warren D.: *Music and Musicians in Ancient Greece*. 1994, Ithaca & London

Aristophanes: "The Acharnians," in: *The Plays of Aristophanes* (Introduction by John P. Maine), Vol. I. 1909/1949, London

Aristophanes: *Acharnerne* (eds. Holger Friis Johansen and Erik H. Madsen). 1955/1977, Copenhagen

Autissier, Anne-Marie (ed.): *The Europe of Festivals. From Zagreb to Edinburgh, Intersecting Viewpoints*. 2009, Paris

Bakhtín, Mikhail: *Rabelais and His World*. 1968, Cambridge, MA

Bennet, Andy (ed.): *Remembering Woodstock*. 2004, Aldershot & Burlington

Bille, Torben (ed.): *Dansk Rockleksikon 1956–2002*. 2002, Copenhagen

Blume, Horst-Dieter: *Einfürung in das antike Theaterwesen*. 1978, Darmstadt

Bodil, Due: "Tragedien," in: *Det græske Teater* (ed. Lise Hannestad). 1985, Århus

Calame, Claude: *Choruses of Young Women in Ancient Greece. Their Morphology, Religious Role, and Social Functions* (New and Revised Edition). 2001 (1977), New York & Oxford (Roma)

Carlson, Marvin: *Performance: A Critical Introduction*. 1996, London & New York

Carson, Anne: "Putting Her in Her Place," in: *Before Sexuality* (eds. David M. Halperin et al.). 1990, NJ

Coleman, Peter: *Shopping Environments – Evolution, Planning and Design*. 2006, Oxford

Comotti, Giovanni: *Music in Greek and Roman Culture*. 1989 (1979), Baltimore & London (Roma)

Conelly, Joan B.: "Parthenon and *Parthenoi*: A Mythological Interpretation of the Parthenon Frieze," *American Journal of Archaeology*, 100, pp. 53–80. 1996, The American Institute of Archaeology

Csapo, Eric: "The Men Who Built the Theatres: Theatropolai, Theatronai, and Arkhitektones," in: *The Greek Theatre and Festivals. Documentary Studies* (ed. Peter Wilson). 2007, Oxford

Csapo, Eric and Slater, William J.: *The Context of Ancient Drama*. 1994, MI

Dahl, Christian: Tragedie og bystat. Om fællesskab og konflikt i Athens dramatiske kultur. 2010, Copenhagen

Danielsen, Esben: *Note about Roskilde Festival to OH.* 2011

D'Avino, Michele: *Pompeibita. Erotismo sacro, agurale e di costume nell'antica città ce polta.* 1993, published in the series Cultura Antica, Naples

Due, Bodil: "Tragedien og dens udvikling," in: *Det græske teater* (ed. Lise Hannestad). 1985, Århus

Dugdale, Eric: *Greek Theatre in Context.* 2008, Cambridge

Encyklopædi, Den Store Danske: *The Great Danish Encyclopedia: The Year Refers to All Posts Throughout the Work.* 1994, Copenhagen

Engels, Friedrich: *Marx/Engels über Kunst und Literatur II* (Ausswahl und Redaktion Manfred Kliem). 1968, Berlin

Erbe, Berit: "Oldtidsteatret," in: *Teatrets historie* (eds. Chr. Ludvigsen og Stephan Kehler). Politikens Håndbøger no. 278. 1962, Copenhagen

Falk, Gerhard and Falk, Ursula A.: *Youth Culture and the Generation Gap.* 2005, USA

Foccroulle, Bernard: "At the Heart of European Identities," in: *The Europe of Festivals. From Zagreb to Edinburgh, Intersecting Viewpoints* (ed. Anne-Marie Autissiers). 2009, Paris

Fock, Eva: *Musik omkring os – om musik i Tyrkiet, Pakistan, Marokko . . . . . og Danmark.* 2005, Copenhagen

Frederiksen, Rune: "The Greek Theatre. A Typical Building in the Urban Center of the Polis?" in: *Even More Studies in the Ancient Greek Polis.* Papers from the Copenhagen Polis Centre 6 (ed. Thomas Heine Nielsen). 2000, Stuttgart

Frith, Simon: *Sound Effects: Youth, Leisure and the Politics of Rock 'n' Roll.* 1981, New York

Garfinkel, Yosef: *Dancing at the Dawn of Agriculture.* 2003, Austin, Texas

Goldhill, Simon and Osborne, Robin (eds.): *Performance Culture and Athenian Democracy.* 1999, Cambridge

Gonzales, Michael Jose: "Nøgenløbet på Roskilde gennem tiden," in: *GAFFA.* 2010, Copenhagen

Green, J.R.: *Theatre in Ancient Greek Society.* 1994, London & New York

Gyldendals Musikhistorie (ed. Knud Ketting). 1982, Copenhagen

Hall, Edith: *The Theatrical Cast of Athens. Interactions Between Ancient Greek & Society.* 2006, Oxford

Hammershøj, Lars Geer: "Selvdannelse og nye former for Socialitet – technofest som eksempel," *Dansk Sociologi,* no. 2/12. 2001, Sociologisk Institut, Copenhagen University, Copenhagen

Hannestad, Lise (ed.): *Det græske Teater.* 1985, Århus

Hansen, Mogens Herman: *Det athenske demokrati – og vores.* 2005, Copenhagen

Harsløf, Olav: "Det autoritære og det antiautoritære – eller livet og lysten," in: *Dansk Pædagogisk Tidsskrift no. 1* (ed. Lars Jakob Muschinsky). 1989, Copenhagen

Harsløf, Olav: *Lysår – kunstens kulturhistorie i Danmark i det 20. århundrede.* 2000, Copenhagen

Harsløf, Olav: "Den producerede teateroplevelse," in: *Theatre-in-Business. Udfordringer og potentialer* (eds. Bethina Louise Røge, Gry Worre Hallberg, Lara Lindinger-Löwy, Maja Topsøe-Jensen and Michael Eigtved). 2011, Copenhagen

Hauser, Arnold: *The Social History of Art*, Vol. I. 1951, London. Reprinted 1989

Heine Nielsen, Thomas: "Olympia and the Classical Hellenic State City-Culture," *Historiske-Filosofiske Meddelelser*, 96. 2007, Copenhagen

Heine Nielsen, Thomas: "The Extent and Significance of the Greek Athletic Culture in the Classical Period," in: *A lecture held at the Danish Institute in Athens.* 2010

Hjortsø, Leo: *Hellas.* 1968, Copenhagen

Hov, Live: *Kvinnerollene i antikkens teater – skrevet, spilt og sett av menn.* 1998, Oslo

Huizinga, Johan: *Homo Ludens: A Study of the Play-Element in Culture.* 1955, Boston

Ingham, James: "Listening Back from Blackbourn: Virtual Sound Worlds and Creation of Temporary Autonomy," in: *Living Through* (ed. Pop. A. Blake). 1999, London & New York

Isager, Signe: "Festerne og opførelserne," in: *Det græske Teater* (ed. Lise Hannestad). 1985, Århus

Jensen, Erik: *På Roskilde.* 2003, Copenhagen

Jensen, Erik: "Slut op om den orange følelse," in: *Politiken.* 2010, Copenhagen

Jensen, Minna Skafte. 2004, Odense

Johansen, Holger Friis: "Teatret og samfundet," in: *Det græske Teater* (ed. Lise Hannestad). 1985, Århus

Johnson, Jr., Robert Bowie (ed.): *The Parthenon Code: Mankind's History in Marble.* 2004, USA

Kaepler, A.E.: "Dance," in: *Folklore, Cultural Performance, and Popular Entertainment* (ed. R. Bauman), pp. 196–202. 1992, Oxford

Keuls, Eva C.: *The Reign of the Phallus. Sexual Politics in Ancient Athens.* 1993, Berkeley

Kirshenblatt-Gimblett, Barbara: "Performance Studies," in: *Rockefeller Foundation, Culture and Creativity.* 1999, www.nyu.edu/classes/bkg/issues/rock2.htm

Laing, Dave: "The Three Woodstocks and the Live Music Scene," in: *Remembering Woodstock* (ed. Andy Bennet). 2004, Aldershot and Burlington

Lang, Michael and George-Warren, Holly: *The Road to Woodstock. From the Man Behind the Legendary Festival.* 2009, New York

Lonsdale, Stephen H.: *Dance and Ritual Play in Greek Religion.* 1973, London

Lund, Allan A.: *I seng med romerne. Køn og sex i det antikke Rom.* 2005, Copenhagen

Madison, D. Soyini: *Critical Ethnography: Method, Ethics, and Performance.* 2005, Los Angeles

Madison, D. Soyini and Hamera, Judith: "Introduction," in: *The Sage Handbook of Performance Studies*, pp. xvi–xvii. 2006, London

Marling, Gitte and Hans, Kiib: *Instant City@Roskilde Festival.* 2009, Aalborg

Mathiesen, Thomas J.: *Apollo's Lyre. Greek Music and Music Theory in Antiquity and the Middle Ages.* 1999, Lincoln & London

Mcgovern, Patric: *Uncorking the Past. The Quest for Wine, Beer and Other Alcoholic Beverage.* 2009, Los Angeles & London

Mejer, Jørgen: "Det klassiske Athen," in: *Verdens Litteraturhistorie* (ed. Hans Hertel), Vol. 1 Oldtiden. 1994, Copenhagen

Metro Xpress is a Danish free newspaper

Munkgård Pedersen, Kristine: *Midlertidige mobiliseringer og flygtige forbindelser – om kulturproduktion på Roskilde Festival.* 2010, www.openarchive.cbs.dk

Naerebout, F.G.: *Attractive Performances. Ancient Greek Dance: Three Preliminary Studies.* 1997, Amsterdam

Negt, Oskar: "68 – tyve år efter," in: *Dansk Pædagogisk Tidsskrift no. 8* (ed. Lars Jakob Muchinsky). 1988, Copenhagen

Nietzsche, Friedrich: "Die Geburt der Tragödie. 1872," in: *Nietzsche Werke. Kritische Ausgabe. Herausgegeben von Giorgio Colli und Mazzino Montinari.* 1972, Berlin

Nietzsche, Friedrich: *The Birth of Tragedy and Other Writings* (eds. Raymond Guess and Ronald Speirs). 1999. Cambridge

Østergaard, Jan Stubbe: "En hvid løgn," in: *Politiken 2.3.* 2004, Copenhagen

Østergaard, Jan Stubbe (ed.): *Tracking Colour. The Polycrome of Greek and Roman Sculpture in the Ny Carlsberg Glyptotek.* Preliminary Report 1. 2009, Copenhagen

Parke, H.W.: *Festival of the Athenians.* 1977, London

Pauly, der neue: *Enzyklopädie der Antike* (eds. Hubert Cancik and Helmuth Schneider). 1996 (the year refers to all posts throughout the work), Stuttgart & Weimar

Paulys Realencyklopädie der classischen Altertumswissenschaft. 1893–1939, Stuttgart

Perlman, Paula: *City and Sanctuary in Ancient Greece. The Theorodokia in the Peloponnese* (ed. Hans-Joachim Gehrke). 2000, published by HYPOMNEMATA – Untersuchungen zur antike und zur ihrem Nachleben. Heft 121, Göttingen

Pickard-Cambridge, Arthur: *The Theatre of Dionysus.* 1946, Oxford

Pickard-Cambridge, Arthur: *The Dramatic Festivals of Athens,* 2nd edition. 1953, Oxford. Revised by J. Gould and D.M. Lewis. 1969, Oxford

Pini, Evi: *One Man – One Period. Pericles and Classical Athens.* 2010, Athens

Reinholdt Nielsen, Per: *Rebel & Remix – rockens historie.* 2003, Copenhagen

Rietveld, Hillegonda: "Living the Dream", in Steve Redhead (ed.) *Rave Off: Politics and Deviance in Contemporary Youth Culture.* 1993, Avebury

Rosivach, Vincent J.: "The System of Public Sacrifice in Fourth-Century Athens," *American Classical Studies,* 34. 1994, USA

Roskilde Festival's Annual Reports: https://roskildefestivalgruppen.dk/da/årsrapporter/

Roskilde Festivals hjemmeside: http://roskilde-festival.dk/historie/

Rou Jensen, Anders: *Mellem drømme & drøn. Roskilde Festival 25 år.* 1995, Copenhagen

Rung, Grethe (ed.): *Vi mødes i Roskilde. Roskilde Festival i 25 år.* 1995, Roskilde

Salmonsens Konversationsleksikon, 2nd edition. 1915–30. Copenhagen

Schechner, Richard: *Performance Theory,* 1977. Second edition, 1988 (Routledge Classics 2003), New York

Schechner, Richard: *Performance Theory,* 2nd edition. 1988 (Routledge Classics 2003), New York

Schechner, Richard: *The Future of Ritual. Writings on Culture and Performance.* 1993, London

Schechner, Richard: *Performance Studies. An Introduction.* 2002, New York

Sennet, Richard: *The Fall of Public Man.* 1976, London

Skov, Leif: "How Fragile We Are," in: *Jul i Roskilde 2001* (ed. Per Schneider). 2001, Roskilde

Tangires, Helen: *Public Market and Civic Culture.* 2008, New York

Thomsen, Ole: "Aristofanes," in: *Det græske Teater* (ed. Lise Hannestad). 1985, Århus

Turner, Victor: *The Ritual Process – Structure and Anti-Structure.* 1969, New York

Turner, Victor: *Dramas, Fields and Metaphors.* 1974, Ithaca

Turner, Victor: *From Ritual to Theater.* 1982, New York

Vagnby, Jes: *Midlertidig arkitektur og fysisk planlægning på Roskilde Festival.* 2010, Copenhagen

VisitDenmark: *Festivalen som trækplaster – en turistøkonomisk undersøgelse af Danmarks største kulturfestival 08.* 2009, Copenhagen

Vitruvius: *On Architecture* (Edited from the Harleian Manuscript 2767 and translated into English by Frank Granger). 1931/1955, London

Vitruvius: *Om Arkitektur. Tio Böker* (In Swedish by Birgitta Dalgren. Commentary Johan Mårtelius). 1989, Stockholm

Vitruvius: *Ten Books on Architecture* (Translation by Ingrid D. Rowland. Commentary and Illustrations by Thomas Noble Howe). 1999, Cambridge

West, Martin Litchfield: *Ancient Greek Music.* 1992, Oxford

White, Dave: http://classicrock.about.com/od/history/a/woodstock_101_.htm

Wiles, David: *Greek Theatre Performance. An Introduction.* 2000, Cambridge

Wiles, David: *A Short History of Western Performance Space.* 2003, Cambridge

Wilson, Peter: "Costing the Dionysia," in: *Performance, Iconography, Reception. Studies in Honour of Oliver Toplin* (eds. Martin Reverman and Peter Wilson). 2008, Oxford

Zarilli, Phillip B.: "Early Drama and Theatre in Context," in: *Theatre Histories. An Introduction* (eds. Phillip B. Zarelli, Bruce McConachie, Gary J. Williams and Carol Fischer Sorgenfrei). 2006, New York & London

Index

For Product Safety Concerns and Information please contact our EU representative GPSR@taylorandfrancis.com
Taylor & Francis Verlag GmbH, Kaufingerstraße 24, 80331 München, Germany

www.ingramcontent.com/pod-product-compliance
Lightning Source LLC
LaVergne TN
LVHW010914110826
845149LV00013B/2362

9781032237824